Origins of an Idea

An Apologetic for Original Expression

Barry Neil Shrum

Introduction by Daymond John

DEDICATION

To my wonderful wife and son, a family who provide me with the
nurturing environment in which to originate my own ideas.
I love you both.

CONTENTS

Everything in creation has its appointed painter or poet and remains in bondage like the princess in the fairy tale 'til its appropriate liberator comes to set it free.

—Ralph Waldo Emerson

ACKNOWLEDGMENTS

There are many people who deserve thanks: to my wife Dawn, who is my constant source of guidance and direction, and to my son Brentyn for his unwavering love and belief; to my good friend Dr. James Wells, Shakespearean professor at Muskingum University for reading my first drafts and giving me valuable feedback; to Gary Terashita for his enthusiasm, guidance and editing skills; to my 2009-2012 copyright classes at Belmont University's Mike Curb School of Music Business for their inquisitiveness, honesty and patience as I worked through many of the book ideas through their lectures; and finally, to deceased father, my mother, and two brothers whose influence molded my world view in my formative years

INTRODUCTION

As an entrepreneur, angel investor and a member of the ABC television show, *Shark Tank*, I see creative execution of original ideas every day. I believe that original ideas are the soul of creativity and the soul of new business. But without the ability to capitalize on our ideas, we risk stripping entrepreneurial spirit out of America. In Origins of an Idea, Mr. Shrum defends the principles that give entrepreneurs, inventors and creators the inspiration to take action and create new businesses - and new ideas - every day. He points out that these principles are so significant to the existence and health of America, they have been drafted into our Constitution. At the very foundation of business and creativity, we are entitled to reap the rewards for our ideas, labor and tenacity. This is an important concept and one that is very dear to my heart.

My parents, particularly my mother, instilled in me very strong ideas about work and reward. I specifically remember a large can opener my mother displayed on our kitchen wall that had the words "Think Big" inscribed on it. Mom used to tell me, "It takes just as much energy to think big as it does to think small." She taught me that working a day job would not make me rich, but rather the inspiration from within, could. She taught me that if I had an idea and I worked hard to see it through, I could achieve anything.

That was a life lesson that was reinforced by growing up in Queens. When I was a teenager, I became aware of a new type of music that everyone around me was listening to. It started with the young kids, this energy of the street: because of the way they would walk around, sort of with a swagger in their step, people started calling this new form of music hip-hop. But hip-hop wasn't just a new type of music you'd listen too; it was something you do, something you live. It was about the way they walked, the way they talked: everything about them. Soon, a local boy named Russell Simmons began driving around the neighborhoods sporting expensive, new cars. Simmons was the creator of Def Jam records and the founder of the hip-hop genre.

Because of his ability to secure a monopoly in their new form of creativity, Simmons was able to succeed, and so were the likes of L.L. Cool Jay and others from the hood.

Creativity breeds creativity. I learned from my Mother and from Simmons that I was no different than any other successful person. I learned that if I had a unique and different idea that met certain need in the market, I could capitalize on that idea and become successful myself. As it ultimately turned out, this new form of music gave me the inspiration for my now famous clothing line, FUBU - for us, by us. I can still remember sewing my first hats in my basement and taking them to the coliseum. I didn't know if anyone would buy them. But I sold $800 worth. Now, my company logo, emblazoned on every piece of clothing we produce, is known worldwide. That intellectual property has served me well, as FUBU's gross profits at its peak exceeded $350 million dollars annually. In fact, in my own book The Brand Within, I maintain that each of us is a brand and that it permeates everything we do.

From my experiences, I learned that with my blood sweat and tears, I made something everything else wanted and I profited from my unique ideas. In his book, Origins of an Idea, Mr. Shrum defends the concept that John Locke taught us a long time ago: people deserve the "fruits of their labor." Any future that supports an environment that allows, encourages and protects an individual's efforts to build their future and their business on original creative ideas and hard work, is a good one.

But there are those in our country, and across the globe, who don't want to support the idea that a person should be rewarded for their labor. The music industry has suffered in the last ten years because people don't believe they should pay the people who make their music. Mr. Shrum gives examples of people who say that all information, including original ideas, should be free for everyone to use. That philosophy is not what made America what it is today.

If the entrepreneurial spirit is to survive - if creators are to be nourished - then we have to listen to the advice in this book and reward our entrepreneurs, our creators, our inventors and, yes, even our artists. We have to let them derive the benefit from exploiting the fruits of their labor. We are all taught in America to "think big." It's time to return to that age old concept of rewarding those who do.

-Daymond John

PROLOGUE

Original ideas, particularly those expressed in the creative arts, are indispensable to the advancement of human knowledge. The protection of such expression is essential to human progress. Our current U.S. copyright construct was conceived to stimulate original expression and, *ipso facto*, be beneficial to society. These basic tenets of American society are being challenged by modern movements threatening to destroy the rights granted us by the Framers of the United States Constitution. What is contained in this volume is my defense of the philosophies and beliefs underlying the institution of copyright.

The current U.S. copyright system is designed, counter-intuitively, to sacrifice some of the needs of the many (society) to the needs of the few (the individual) with the expectation that sharing original thoughts will ultimately contribute to social dialogue and thereby benefit society. Creation and innovation is directed at the advancement of human knowledge, or what I will refer to as the "continuum of knowledge." Our Founding Fathers viewed the trade-off as an acceptable compromise given the perceived benefits.

Despite this well-crafted and grounded construct that is copyright, there are people who want us to believe the ubiquity of free digital information on the Internet somehow negates the need for protection of original expression through what they characterize as a selfish system of copyright monopoly. The implied assumption is that the system of establishing an incentive to authors and inventors to encourage them to create no longer benefits society. I question that assumption.

More discomforting to me, however, is the underlying assumption in this movement that says it is no longer possible to have an original idea; that all new innovations borrow from some preceding idea. This trend in thought threatens to destroy the Constitutional foundation for intellectual property laid by the delegates to the Constitutional convention. Built on the backs of the Enlightenment philosophers, our Forefathers anticipated that the grant of rights would be an incentive to creators and thereby generate a free flowing marketplace of ideas. Later, the Supreme Court would aptly describe copyright as the "engine of free expression." So, in contrast to these antagonists, I agree with the Founding Fathers that original ideas fuel the drive in human innovation toward a better future. As a society, it is time to refocus the debate, drawing our inspiration from the faith of our Founding Fathers in the creativity of our nation, and to defend the rights they gave us. We dare not let original thought become extinct, for if it does, so too will the spark of creativity smolder and fade into the darkness of mediocrity.

As someone who has worked in the field of entertainment and intellectual property law, primarily the music industry, for over 20 years, I have a degree of qualification entitling me to make these observations. In addition to my transactional work in this area, I have also litigated many copyright infringement actions in my years as a lawyer. So, my chosen emphasis naturally includes an intense study of copyright, an area of law I enjoy and a subject I began teaching at Belmont University's Mike Curb School of Music Business in the fall of 2009. It is an issue on which I frequently lecture in my classrooms and write in my blog entries. Finally, as a drummer, writer and artist, I have a deep passion for creative expression. Copyright is the fertile soil producing creativity, which in turn feeds society's needs.

There is little question in the mind of any serious researcher that the past ten years in the music industry are accurately described as the "lost decade" because of rampant, illegal downloading of digital recordings. Such widespread activity, whether you believe it be infringing or not, severely diminished the market for physical product. Hopefully, by the time you finish this book, you will believe that kind of activity to be contrary to society's mores and contrary to society's interests.

But what is more disturbing to me than the loss of revenue to the creators during that ten-year drought is how many in our society devalue the importance of *original thought* and question the uniqueness, and even the existence, of a previously unexpressed idea, or more accurately, thought. Some, in fact, claim our society has achieved such heights, and our population growth has reached such a level, that every conceivable idea has been previously expressed. Of course, every generation thinks theirs is the greatest and most prolific, as is evidenced by the statement attributed to King Solomon long ago, "there is nothing new under the sun." What is different about the most recent trend is that it threatens to shred to fibers the fabric that is a copyright monopoly. That would destroy the benefits to society that our Forefathers envisioned. It would thrust us backward in history to the 1600's when very few creative artists were given an outlet for exploiting their creation.

The phenomenon of devaluing original thought impacts America's creative community in a profound way. In the case of music, the songwriter is directly impacted. When digital product is distributed over peer to peer networks for free, or similarly over BitTorrent sites such as Pirate Bay, it is not surprising that the value of the physical product declines significantly. None of us desire to pay money for something that can be obtained for nothing. For the songwriter, this means he or she receives less mechanical and performances royalties as compared to what they may have received ten years ago. It also means the value of the songwriters' existing catalog of songs decreases, because the value of his or her collected works is based on an accrued and averaged historical net revenue over the past few years. Therefore, if the income decreases, so too does the value of the catalog. The songwriter loses money on many levels.

But the impact of digitization on creative art is not limited to music. In addition to the impact on the income of the lowly songwriter, digitization has affected the revenue of almost all creative souls: painters, sculptures, photographers, authors, and graphic designers. Copyrighted photographs and images of paintings can be "snipped" from the Internet and "Photoshoped," greatly reducing any commercial value they once had. Works of literature are readily copied and read in digital form, reducing the need to purchase a physical copy.

The impact of digitization on creative thought will not stop with the copyrights embodied in CDs, photographs, paintings and books; it will soon spread to patented goods and thus detract from retail sales. "3-D printing" technology is beginning to reach the mainstream with sites such as Thingiverse.com: when that happens manufactured retail products - the so-called "physibles" - will suffer the same fate as digital music. They too will be pirated and given away to the willing for free to anyone who navigates the digital high seas. Strip away the embodiment of the original thought produced by these creators and replace it with mere digits - zeros and ones - and perfect duplications of their works can be produced literally at the touch of button.

Once again, while such infringement of the reproduction right in copyrights disturbs me, it is the philosophy of many of the pirates who do it I find so very abominable. The sense of entitlement expressed by some who are willing to take the property of others is reprehensible. Many feel entitled to download music, movies, and photographs - anything they desire - without any thought about the creators' intellectual property rights; without any thought of the very real people who are being affected by their action. In fact, one blogger boldly suggested he should be rewarded for his infringing activity:

> "I refuse to feel guilty for downloading and sharing music. Every time I listen to a song, or share it with a friend, I'm doing the labels a favor. One that eventually I should be paid for [sic]."

Even the legendary artist/songwriter Neil Young described piracy as the "new radio" because it is "how music gets around." This led Mathew Ingram, the blogger citing the Young comment, to the conclusion that "'piracy' can actually be good for business." Neil Young notwithstanding, it is contrary to my world view to believe that all people can be so callous and uninformed as to believe they are actually making money for the creators by stealing their creations or creating a better business. Such concepts and conclusions are unnatural.

Rather than suffering from mere callousness or ignorance, however, many antagonists are perhaps best described as persistently aggressive in their insistent that they have an inherent right to take any copyrighted work they please. In 2006, a political party, now known as The Pirate Party, was established under the leadership of Rick Falkvinge in Sweden. One of the primary tenants of the political party is that information should be free, specially including, of course, copyright musical works as well as movies. This comes as no surprise when you realize many of the founders of the party were also responsible for one of the leading infringing sites on the Web, the BitTorrent tracker, The Pirate Bay.

But the icing on the cake came in December 2011 when Swedish Legal, Financial, and Administrative Services Agency sanctioned the harebrained idea of Gustav Nipe, a student of Falkvinge, to establish the "Missionary Church of Kopimism," a "religious" institution whose primary belief is that copying is not just a right, but serves a "higher purpose." Copying information without the permission of its creators, in other words, is viewed as an "ethically correct" and "sacred" act under this distorted from of religion. Other beliefs purport the internet is "holy," and Copy+C and Copy+V, the generic computer commands for copy and paste, are considered "sacred symbols." Not surprisingly, The Pirate Bay now operates under the umbrella of this newly-formed church. The attitudes of these obvious and unabashed schemers are perhaps best described as overzealous pride.

The attitude that infringing activities are not only something one should not be ashamed of, but rather socially moral, is reinforced and in some instances underwritten by professors at Ivy League institutions such as Dr. Lawrence Lessig of Harvard University who tells those who would use others' creative works at their whim -- without compensation of course -- their behavior is not only acceptable, but is something that should be sanctioned as part of culture. Lessig teaches "culture always borrows from the past" and therefore all ideas should be free for the present culture to use as they see fit. In fact, Lessig extols the virtues of a "remix culture" that uses the illegally obtained works to create "mash-ups" and "remixes" - collages of copyrighted images, sound recordings and/or videos - embodying direct copies of protected material. These are the videos and songs used on YouTube and other websites that usually include an almost humorous apologetic disclaimer, "no copyright infringement intended."

Lessig's argument follows this logic: we can't stop those who illegally download someone's copyright in order to create their remix, "we can only criminalize them," thus we should simply make such activity legal thereby eliminating the problem. This reminds me of the same logic used by the drug culture of the 60's to support the legalization of marijuana. In fact one blogger, Andy Baio, drew the analogy clearly, suggesting copyright's application to the remix culture is this century's version of prohibition.

This reminds me of something Fyodor Dostoyevsky said, "man has such a predilection for systems and abstract deductions that he is ready to distort the truth intentionally . . . ready to deny the evidence of his senses only to justify his logic." Do we really want to follow Lessig's suggestion and abolish the concept of protecting original thought, only to substitute the pedestrian thoughts of a Twitter feed or the banal dancing babies on YouTube? Do we really want to follow the approach taken by Sweden and make illegal infringement a form of religion? Some may say Lessig is only facing reality and is part of the solution, but many of his ideas are reincarnated in the tenants of the Missionary Church of Kopimism, including the idea that remixing is an expression of faith in the church. Thus, Lessig's suggestion we legalize the infringement in the case of remix seems extreme and it most certainly doesn't allow the core philosophies of copyright to inform the solution.

Other scholars have introduced "new" methods for dealing with the problem of digitization in our society. In an article titled "Legally Speaking: Too Many Copyrights," Pamela Samuelson argues that because of social networking technologies and the prevalence of email, the universe of copyright is expanding at an uncontrollable rate and should be curtailed. Samuelson fears with all the copyrights being created for Twitter feeds, email correspondence, and Facebook walls, we simply cannot protect it all. She proposes an "opt-in" system, which is essentially a return to the registrations formalities that existed under the 1909 act, as a means to allow extensive protections to attach only to those creations whose authors "opt-in" to copyright protection. While this may seem a plausible solution at first glance, a return to the draconian requirements of 1909 is a step backward in the evolution of copyright protection and does not serve the intended purpose well. Surely there is a better solutions to the problem.

One law review author goes further to the extreme than both Lessig and Samuelson, actually describing the current copyright laws as "harmful" and "unconstitutional." The anonymous blogger, PolicyMic, titled one of his posts "Internet Piracy is Not the Problem: It's Time to Eliminate Intellectual Property." PolicyMic's statement of an increasingly prominent trend in thought reaches even further into the abyss. He concludes intellectual property is an antiquated concept that either should be eliminated or, at the very least, gutted of any real enforcement effort. Either way, it is the creative community struck once again, deprived of any economic incentive to create. As we will find out in later chapters, his suggestions eliminate the utilitarian compromise achieved by the Copyright clause and eviscerate its desired incentives.

Warped solutions such as this are not limited to the opinions of online bloggers. Another good example of the idea can be found in the writings of a pair of economists, Michele Boldrin & David K. Levine, who wrote a seminal work, *Against Intellectual Monopoly*, clearly expressing the same sentiment as PolicyMic, *i.e.,* we should do away with the whole lot of intellectual properties, including copyright:

The basic theme of this book is that intellectual monopoly - patents, copyrights, and restrictive licensing agreements - should be swept away.

Boldrin and Levine continue this thought with the bold, unproven assertion ". . . *most innovations have taken place without the benefit of intellectual property.*" In order to support such a tenuous claim, the authors have to assume "most innovations" of mankind occurred prior to the 4th Century, the time the Jewish Talmud first recognized the concept of intellectual property, and perhaps even earlier than that. Jewish laws were stricter than even U.S. laws, allowing absolutely no copyright, even for educational or scientific purposes.

Such sentiments and conclusions expressed so fervently against intellectual property do more harm than good to our creative community. They add insult to the injury already suffered by creators as a result of the rampant piracy with which we are all now so very familiar and to which many have simply become immune. These antagonists seem oblivious to most of the tenets of the Framers of the Copyright Clause and ignorant to the dual purpose of our Constitutional right to a copyright monopoly: to fuel the engine of free speech and to populate the continuum of thought.

Examining the quotations sufficiently illustrates the very foundation and purpose of copyright is under direct attack. The attack intensifies when one peruses the Internet for various discussions regarding the topic. Such a search yields articles and opinions written by "copyleft" advocates and proud "pirates" or "mash up" artists extolling the virtues of piracy and remixing, and ridiculing those who would support the rights of the creators. Often laced with emotive terms, misleading analogies, and misinformation, these diatribes nonetheless significantly and negatively impact the current social Zeitgeist. They have an impact on societal thought which must be countered by balance.

The final provocation for me was a poignant example of this type of misdirection found in an entry recently appearing on the "Green Pirate" blog. Written by an anonymous poster, as many of these tirades often are, it was titled "Evolution Expert Explains Why Piracy is More Important Than Copyright." The title of the blog entry was referring to a recent speech given by Mark D. Pagel, a leading author and expert on evolution. The subject of the speech was not copyright, of course, but cumulative cultural adaptation. In that speech, Dr. Pagel made a statement appealing to the personal aims of the blog author. Pagel commented "as our societies get larger and larger, there's no need, in fact, there's even less of a need for any one of us to be an innovator, whereas there is a great advantage for most of us to be copiers, or followers."

From this statement, the author of the blog draws the erroneous and misguided conclusion that piracy is more important than copyright to society, because stealing ideas gives the pirate "access to more information than those who restrict themselves to authorized channels." Finally, the author concludes that *Internet piracy itself is innovation*. It provides a service that has no competition among authorized distribution channels which operate under *the old paradigm that copying is harmful*." Make sure you understand what this writer is saying: internet piracy is original thought! In other words, stealing an idea is the equivalent of creating it. In a later chapter, I will examine similar claims raised by Brent Gaylor in his film titled *RIP: Remix Manifesto*, in which he argues the work of his favorite mash-up artist, GirlTalk, though direct, infringing copies of original works, are uniquely Girltalk's creations. All of this flies in the face of intuition, common sense, and our innate sense of justice. It just feels wrong.

Anti-copyright sentiments like these appear not only in random places on the Internet, but in legal arguments in cases across the United States. One came to the surface in *Eldred v. Ashcroft*, 537 U.S. 186 (2003), a Supreme Court case brought in opposition to the Copyright Term Extension Act. Similar sentiments also surfaced in the recent grassroots movement that developed online in opposition to legislative initiatives designed to protect the rights of copyright owners, such as the Combating Online Infringement and Counterfeits Act (COICA), the Stop Online Piracy Act (SOPA) and the Preventing Real Online Threats to Economic Creativity and Theft of Intellectual Property Act (PROTECT-IP or PIPA). Most recently in 2012, advocates attacked the efforts of Congress to restore foreign works to the public domain in order to remain compliant with the Uruguay Roundtable Agreement Act in the Supreme Court case *Golan v. Holder*, 132 S.Ct. 873, 565 U.S. _____ (2012), an attack the Supreme Court rejected. Organizations and movements like the Electronic Frontier Foundation, the Creative Commons and the so-called "copy-left" society, Kopimism - many times the instigators of and funding sources for legal actions such as these - provide further and emphatic evidence of this current trend of thought against the concept of original expression.

When an issue reaches such apexes of commerce, of course, the social dialogue is frequently fueled by misinformation too often seeded by well-funded lobbying efforts and/or corporate conglomerates with ulterior financial motives. This fuels opponents to fight back. The U.S. Chamber of Commerce supported the SOPA legislation in 2011, for example, while Google funded a grassroots uprising in opposition ultimately stalling the legislation in the 112th Congress. Often, this type of biased support leads to dialogue from the copyright antagonists couched in misleading terminology, describing those in favor of copyright as "the establishment," "content owners" or "media conglomerates." Often, claims such as "censorship" and "free speech" violations are alleged, as well. Sometimes, "evil" conglomerates are identified by name, such as those opposition efforts our society has witnessed against Disney or Warner Brothers or the lists of SOPA supporters posted on various websites. In the midst of the debate on SOPA, Wikipedia and other influential sites actually blocked access to content to illustrate their alleged belief the act would "break the Internet." The hacker group, Anonymous, threatens destructive actions against companies supporting any viewpoint contrary to their own. Emotive terms and drastic actions such as these merely fuel illogical thought and, unfortunately, either create really bad laws or block beneficial ones. In the end, the debate gets lost in the drama and the very real issues do not get properly and adequately addressed.

Alas, there is never any support for the creative population in these heated debates. The emotional rhetoric ignores the creative soul and obfuscates the real sobering issue in our society today: protection for the creative arts is withering. As our Forefathers envisioned when they created the construct of a copyright monopoly, without the incentive to labor in the fields and harvest it, the fruit of art dies on the vine. It is a construct I, for one, believe still functions quite well and can serve us as a nation for years to come.

As a creative soul myself, as well as student of the Constitution and copyright history, such attacks on the Copyright Clause generally, and on the concept of original expression specifically, bring my blood to a boil. It angers me when Sweden sanctions a religion teaching it is sacred to violate my Constitutional rights and recklessly infringe my creative product. Such an outrage against our country's innate beliefs stimulates me to enlist my skills of theological apologetics to defend the faith of our Founding Fathers. I feel the urge to quote the likes of Jefferson, Madison, Locke, Hobbes, and yes, even C.S. Lewis. The fervent opinion of the logician in my head is that much of the current thought contradicts logic in general and evidences a specific widespread misunderstanding of the copyright construct envisioned and written by the delegates to the Constitutional Convention. More to the point, such aggressive and callous opinions slowly chip away at what I believe to be the origins of an idea. A call to action arises in my very soul and it makes me want to stand in a pulpit and preach it!

So, inspired by my earlier days as a theologian, I drew the subtitle - *an apologetic of original expression* - from my studies of early Christian apologists who defended their faith against their critics; so too, I feel compelled to offer an apologetic for original expression. Copyright needs an advocate against this inexplicable and overwhelming tide of opposition. The debate needs an injection of logic; as Leonard Nimoy once said as Commander Spock on Star Trek, "Logic is the beginning of wisdom, not the end." Although I may not be the most eloquent advocate, the fuel driving my desire to write this defense must be ignited.

As C.S. Lewis observed in his final interview with Sherwood Eliot Wirt, "Writing comes as a result of a very strong impulse, and when it does come, I for one must get it out." So, in the tradition of Socrates and the apologists, I feel the impulse to explore the origins of an idea and to defend original expression. I feel, as it were, the need to "get it out."

ORIGINS OF AN IDEA

CHAPTER 1
New Wine

People don't pour new wine into old wineskins.
If they do, the wine will make the skins burst,
and both the wine and the skins will be ruined.

-Mark 2:22

Article 1, Section 8, Clause 8 of the United States Constitution is the most precise starting point for any discussion of intellectual property and in this specific case, copyright law. In it, our Forefathers gave Congress the right to establish a monopoly in favor of authors and inventors for the express purpose of promoting the "progress of science and useful arts."

Dictionaries contemporaneous with the time of our country's founding defined "progress" as "advancement in knowledge" and as "passage from one place to another." So, in their expressed intent to promote progress, the Framers of our Constitution had in mind a larger societal benefit by offering this encouragement for the creative laborers to share the "fruits of their labor": they recognized that by giving over some of their rights of free speech, society would gain an immensely fertile breeding ground for ideas. By doing so, the Framers intended to move the country from a new world lacking in widespread knowledge and education toward a world of advanced knowledge in which innovation and creativity flourished. The only means they knew to do this was to provide encouragement for people to create in exchange for society giving up any rights in those original ideas. This incentive system - a "fair trade" if you will - has served our society well for over 200 years.

Not all of our Founding Fathers were initially supportive of the concept, however. The merits and justifications for granting this monopoly were not immediately obvious to those who witnessed and studied the history of Queen Elizabeth's who granted letters patents as if they were going out of style. This practice of granting monopolies to favored parties actually curtailed competition and suppressed creativity, or so it would seem to those opposed. So, the subject of monopolies was apparently the subject of considerable debate, particularly among the likes of Thomas Jefferson, James Madison, and Charles Pinckney. Their debates spilled over into the topics bantered about among the remaining delegates to the Constitutional convention, who spent a week long session in August 1787 discussing various proposals enumerating the powers of Congress.

But in the end there was little debate: our forward-thinking ancestors recognized the importance of disseminating information throughout the newly formed republic, even if it meant giving up some of society's rights to freely use ideas, because encouraging the widespread dissemination of knowledge was necessary in order to preserve democracy. They felt the weight of responsibility inherent in creating a new nation and believed they could learn from the mistakes of the past and initiate a better system. As John Adams observed, a monopoly in "property must be secured or liberty cannot exist." This holds true for intellectual property as well as real property, perhaps even more so. This connection between property and liberty is crucial in comprehending the importance of the copyright monopoly in today's society as well.

Jefferson was perhaps one of the staunchest proponents of limiting governmental monopolies, not only with regard to intellectual property but *in all respects*. Jefferson was so opposed to monopolies he was in favor of drafting a clause in the Constitution that prohibited all types. He once declared:

> I have sworn upon the altar of God eternal hostility against every form of tyranny over the mind of man.

On the face of it, it seems the concept of granting a monopoly in an original thought flew in the face of every tenet for which Jefferson stood. As noted earlier, he witnessed many government tyrannies and studied the atrocities befalling England at the hands of King James, King Charles the I and II, and Queen Elizabeth. The letters patent granting a monopoly in publishing to the Stationers' Company served as a tool of censorship for over a hundred years, inspiring the polemical tract of John Milton, *Areopagitica* which denounced the system. This is a piece of literature I'm certain Jefferson read. There is no doubt Jefferson was an avid student of history and as such, had a very difficult time wrapping his brain around Madison's insistence on granting a monopoly in original thoughts, even for such noble, utilitarian goals.

With regard to the subject of ideas in particular, Jefferson said in his indubitably prosaic way,

> If nature has made any one thing less susceptible than all others of exclusive property, it is the action of the thinking power called an idea. . . . [S]he made them . . . incapable of confinement or exclusive appropriation.

In the conclusion to this correspondence, Jefferson opined that "Inventions then cannot, *in nature*, be a subject of property." But as we will later discover, this quotation should not be taken out of the context of the natural law versus utilitarian debate in which it was intended. It would be a mistake to read too much into Jefferson's words here.

Jefferson's most frequent debate partner was his old friend James Madison, with whom he had the most spirited exchanges through their correspondence. Among other things, they of course discussed the limited monopoly of intellectual property.

With specific regard to governmental monopolies of any kind, as noted, Jefferson was initially opposed to the concept with a vengeance and expressed this on numerous occasions to his old friend, even months after the Constitutional Convention ended. Unable to attend the convention, Jefferson felt the need to have his views represented. For example, in a letter to Madison drafted on July 31, 1788, perhaps in connection with the ratification of the newly signed Constitution, Jefferson penned these words specifically in reference to the copyright monopoly:

> The saying there shall be no monopolies lessens the incitements to ingenuity, which is spurred on by the hope of a monopoly for a limited time, as of 14 years;

> *but the benefit even of limited monopolies is too doubtful to be opposed to that of their general suppression.* (Emphasis added).

As he observed here in the emphasized sentence, Jefferson thought the evils of establishing a monopoly by governmental fiat far outweighed any benefits of a limited monopoly to "incite ingenuity," even if the monopoly only had a duration of 14 years. Even as the Constitution was being ratified, Jefferson still had doubts about government-granted monopolies.

In James Madison's pointed response, dated October 17, 1788, he agrees in principle with Jefferson's opposition to monopolies in general, but defended the specific concept of a copyright monopoly as a necessity which he championed, and one which should be supported:

"*With regard to monopolies they are justly classed among the greatest nuisances in government.* But is it clear that as encouragements to literary works and ingenious discoveries, they are not too valuable to be wholly renounced? Would it not suffice to reserve in all cases a right to the public to abolish the privilege at a price to be specified in the grant of it? Is there not also infinitely less danger of this abuse in our governments than in most others? *Monopolies are sacrifices of the many to the few.* Where the power is in the few it is natural for them to sacrifice the many to their own partialities and corruptions. Where the power, as with us, is in the many not in the few, the danger cannot be very great that the few will be thus favored. It is much more to be dreaded that the few will be unnecessarily sacrificed to the many."

Evident in Madison's response to Jefferson are many of the cornerstones upon which the United States' construction of a copyright monopoly are built, not the least of which is that monopolies, in general, are a "nuisance" whenever exercised by the government. Notwithstanding this general disdain, however, Madison emphasizes the counterintuitive idea that an individual monopoly in intellectual property benefits society when he states that the most important seminal principle is that "monopolies are sacrifices of the many to the few."

In the salutation of the letter, Madison also wisely prophesied the present state of affairs in which creative people suffer at the hands of a majority given too much control. He says *"the danger cannot be very great that the few will be thus favored. It is much more to be dreaded that the few will be unnecessarily sacrificed to the many."* Unfortunately, the few, *i.e.*, the creators, are currently being sacrificed for the whims of the many who want all information, regardless of ownership rights, to be free; they are dying on the shores of The Pirate Bay.

That Madison strongly believed a monopoly was necessary to extend knowledge throughout the newly developing nation is expressed even more clearly in a letter he wrote to W.T. Barry in 1822, in which he stated the "American people owe it to themselves, and to the cause of free government" to promote "the advancement and diffusion of knowledge." That sentiment is even truer in the digital world of today.

While Madison's words to Barry at first may appear contrary to the utilitarian principles which he and Jefferson studied and to which they primarily adhered, *i.e.*, that what was good for the many was good for the few, after careful consideration, it becomes clear they perfectly align. Specifically, in regard to the copyright monopoly, sacrificing the needs of the many to the needs of the few, *i.e., allowing the monopoly,* was intrinsically valuable *so long as* it meant the few would be encouraged to create "literary works and ingenious discoveries" which would be accessible by the collective society. Notice how Madison takes what at first seems anti-utilitarian, giving a monopoly to the few, and turns it around into a utilitarian construct.

The way Madison envisioned the copyright construct, the societal benefit occurs not only when a work is reclaimed by society through the public domain, but also, and perhaps more critically, when the work is initially released to the public for general consumption. For the developing New World, the moment a new work was released into circulation was the moment society began to benefit. There was no need to wait until it fell into the public domain. We will later see this is a concept Madison probably derived from John Locke's *Second Treatise on Civil Government.* Because these results benefitted society tremendously, Madison correctly observed, in the end, this somewhat natural-law view was actually more aligned with his utilitarian bent. This paradox of a tradeoff is perhaps ultimately what convinced Jefferson of the general value of a monopoly in creations, for he too was a student of Locke and a master of philosophy.

For reasons not clear from the factual record, the concerns about the government granting rights of property to creators of intellectual property to the exclusion of others, as expressed by Jefferson, were ultimately incorporated into the Constitution, not by Madison, but by Charles Pinckney in his proposal to the Convention regarding this issue. Perhaps Jefferson expressed similar thoughts to Mr. Pinckney. Regardless, Pinckney's penultimate clause, "to secure to authors exclusive rights *for a limited time*, added the infamous limitation phrase to similar proposals drafted by Madison. In the end, it was a combination of their drafts that was ultimately used by the Committee of Detail to draft the final clause which included the "for a limited time" phraseology that has been the subject of much debate in recent years. But this limitation does not change the balancing of interests between society and the individual in the least. The clause was passed by the Convention members with very little, if any debate.

The First Congress of the United States also understood the balancing of interests involved and was well aware of the concerns debated by Madison and Jefferson. When they exercised the powers granted to them in the Constitution to pass the U.S.'s first Copyright Act in 1790, they subtitled the legislation "An act for the encouragement of learning." In their journal entries regarding the passage of the act, Congress indicated "the promotion of science and literature will contribute to the security of a free Government. . . ." George Washington reiterated this understanding in his address to both houses of Congress in 1790:

> . . . there is nothing which can better deserve your patronage
> than the promotion of science and literature. Knowledge is . .
> . the surest basis of public happiness.

These words of Congress and our first president are clearly echoes of earlier conversations with Jefferson and Madison. They give us vivid expressions of the overall goal of our current copyright monopoly.

As with most great thinkers, Jefferson often mulled over ideas upon which he previously reached a resolution. Despite the efforts of those who addressed Jefferson's concerns about the subject of monopolies with the "limited times" provision, as adopted by the Convention on September 17, 1787, Jefferson was an obstinate soul and so still was not entirely convinced. His fastidiousness is apparent in a subsequent letter from Jefferson to Madison dated August 28, 1789, in which he regrets a lack of further refinement in the Constitutional language adopted at the Convention:

> I like the declaration of rights as far as it goes, but I should have been for going further. For instance, the following alterations and additions would have pleased me. . . Article 9. Monopolies may be allowed to persons for their own productions in literature, and their own inventions in the arts, for a term not exceeding ___ years, but for no longer term, and for no other purpose.

These thoughts may have been inspired by Congress' consideration of the proposed legislation that ultimately became the first U.S. Copyright Law, passed less than a year later in 1790. This is suggested by later correspondence in which Jefferson filled in the blank with a suggested term of 19 years based on the average life span of a person at the time. When Congress enacted the first law, they actually adopted a shorter term of 14 years. Jefferson's suggestion that the copyright monopoly be limited to the average life of a person was based on his assumption it should not be willed to future generations. As he explained, "the earth belongs . . . to the living; that the dead have neither powers nor right over it."

Note Jefferson's prophetic observation here that the monopoly should only be provided to individuals "for their own productions . . . and inventions . . . and for no other purpose." If Jefferson had his way - and he did with the first iteration of the clause - the copyright monopoly could only be possessed by persons during their lifetime and only for "their own" creations. This limitation is, arguably, inherent in the language of the clause as it was drafted, stating that Congress shall have the right to "secure to" authors and inventors the rights to "their creations." Obviously, under the current copyright construct, our jurisprudence and legislative interpretations have negated that particular limitation and extended the right to a creator's heirs, or any other transferees, for at least 70 years. Ultimately, the Supreme Court gave Congress broad latitude to interpret the "for limited times" language, as long as it is limited in some way.

We should observe here that after some years passed and Jefferson had the benefit of experience rather than mere philosophical conjecture upon which to draw his observations, he ultimately grew more and more comfortable with this practice of granting governmental monopolies to creators. The fact Jefferson ultimately bought into Madison's insightful arguments, that the copyright monopoly serves an important social utility, is witnessed in a letter written by Jefferson during his second term to Mr. Oliver Evans, an inventor with several patents for milling flour, carding wool, refrigeration, and for a steam-carriage design.

The letter in reference is dated May 2, 1807, in response to a letter from Evans in which he ostensibly expressed some concern over the validity of one of his recently-approved patent, likely related to his steam engine, although neither the correspondence nor the court specifies. Jefferson assured Mr. Evans a technical oversight by his lawyer would likely not invalidate his patent.

As it turned out, in fact, Mr. Evans' patent did expire, and Jefferson, Madison, and the Congress stepped in to rectify the situation through the rare passage of a special law entitled "an act for the relief of Oliver Evans," which the Supreme Court upheld in *Evans v. Jordan & Morehead*, 13 U.S. 199 (1815). In the letter's conclusion, Jefferson expresses this sentiment:

> Nobody wishes more than I do that ingenuity should receive a liberal encouragement: *nobody estimates higher the utility which society has derived from that [ingenuity] displayed by yourself*; and I assure you with truth that I shall always be ready to manifest by every service I can render you.

The length to which then President Jefferson went to extend protection for Mr. Evans' unjustly unprotected invention for the sake of its benefit to society speaks volumes. Over the years, Madison's ideology and influence apparently convinced Jefferson of the efficacy of the monopoly in copyright and patents in securing a "utility" for society, despite his own earlier words that "inventions cannot, in nature, be the subject of property."

Even more specifically, in correspondence to Isaac McPherson in 1813, Jefferson supported the granting of a limited monopoly right, but only "as an encouragement to men to pursue ideas which may produce utility." At long last, Jefferson and Madison were marching to the beat of the same Revolutionary drum.

As was Jefferson, even the copyright antagonists, Boldrin & Levine, who were cited earlier are ultimately forced to confess the wisdom of the monopoly construct developed by our friends Pinckney and Madison, despite their impassioned opposition to intellectual property monopolies. In a rare admission by a scholar that their entire work may be, in fact, mere dribble, they sheepishly admit:

> . . . while expounding the theory of competitive innovation, we also recognize that under perfect competition, some socially desirable innovations will not be produced. When this is the case, *monopoly power may generate the necessary incentive for the putative innovator to introduce socially valuable goods. And the value for society of these goods could dwarf the social losses we have documented. So, by our own admission, it is a theoretical possibility that intellectual monopoly could, at the end of the day, be better than competition.* . .(Emphasis added).

Such brutal honesty is refreshing, as is the recognition that the construct of Madison is a worthy one. And so the philosophical underpinnings built by the utilitarian's, then John Locke, and their progeny, have continued to permeate and support the U.S. concept of a copyright monopoly over the years, even as it has evolved in attempts to meet new technologies as they develop. All who have examined the issue, from Madison on down throughout history to Boldrin & Levine, have witnessed its efficiency.

Under the authority granted to them in Article 1, Section 8, Clause 8 of the Constitution, for example, Congress has throughout the years established varied limitations on the monopoly of copyright in order to maintain the balance anticipated by Madison and inspired by Locke. In the first U.S. copyright law of 1790, as noted earlier, authors were ultimately limited to a 14 year monopoly, plus the option to extend the monopoly for a second 14 year term. In the present construct, authors are limited to a monopoly for the duration of their life, plus an additional seventy years in which their families and/or heirs can exercise the monopoly. These limitations, according to the Supreme Court, fall well within the scope of the "limited times" envisioned by the Constitution.

In addition to these time limitations and in the spirit of Thomas Jefferson, Congress has also imposed other limitations on the monopoly of copyright over the years. For example, originally, the copyright monopoly only applied to "useful knowledge" produced by society, by which they primarily meant writings and inventions. With regard to the "writings" component, this limitation evolved and expanded over the years into what we now understand as the definition of a copyright, *i.e.*, an original idea expressed in a tangible format for more than a transitory duration.

Other limitations, such as the first sale doctrine and fair use, are not pertinent to the point here, but should be observed in the context of how they serve as limitations on creators' rights, a point which will be discussed in more detail later.

Throughout U.S. history then, these limitations on the monopoly of copyright have, as intended by our Forefathers, served to create a very delicate balance between the needs of the few and the needs of the many. On the "few" side of the balance scale, we place our desire to incentivize authors and inventors to populate the marketplace of ideas with individual creations. On the other side of the scale we place the utilitarian goal of populating a free market exchange of those ideas for the good of society. This balance reflects the fact that providing exclusive rights to authors and inventors encourages their creation of new works, but can also inhibits the progress of knowledge and learning by restricting access to existing works. The second part of the balance - the marketplace of ideas - is what has evolved to encompass the "public domain" concept of copyright law. But it is important to note the emphasis of our Founding Fathers was not on the public domain. As illustrated earlier, Madison and his colleagues believed the benefit to society actually arose immediately after the newly creative work was distributed by its author. This is an important point often obscured by the current trend to focus on the lack of works in the public domain.

The petitioner's brief in the recent Supreme Court case *Golan v. Holder* is a good illustration of this misplaced focus on the public domain as the center of society's benefits. The petitioner described the public domain as a:

> time-honored tradition of preserving and expanding the public domain makes the products of learning, knowledge and creativity widely available and free to all for any purpose. It also helps expand that body of knowledge by providing the building blocks of future creativity in music, art, entertainment and literature. The public domain promotes the diffusion of knowledge, and provides the raw material to expand it.

This idea of a public domain as described here and as it is commonly understood today thus includes *both* "products of learning, knowledge and creativity" that have lost copyright protection and the "building blocks of future creativity in music, art, entertainment and literature" which are free for every person to utilize. This is an erroneous equivocation of the two components. While the public domain as understood today may include both components, I think it likely that our Forefathers would have viewed them more independently.

The idea of a public domain most likely dates back to the Roman Empire and its concepts of *res communes, res publicae* and *res universitatis*. The phrase res communes referred to those things that are commonly enjoyed by all living beings as necessities of life, such as air, light, water, space, symbols, musical notes, and, yes, even ideas. The other two phrases specifically referred, respectively, to anything that was shared by society and anything that was owned by a municipality. If our Forefathers had any understanding of some independent class of works that existed in an independent "public domain," it was not apparent in the Copyright Clause or in the 1790 Copyright Act, contrary to the arguments of the petitioner in *Golan v. Holder*, who specifically state Congress "created the public domain . . . when it enacted the first copyright statute in 1790." If this is true, Congress only did so implicitly, not directly, because one can find no reference to the importance of a public domain in the House Record surrounding the passage of this Act. That is not to say unprotected works did not exist and *ipso facto* would have been part of the public domain. That is axiomatic. But it is important to understand that the first *direct* reference to the concept of a public domain in the annals of the United States Congress did not appear until the language of the 1909 Act was drafted over almost 120 years later, wherein it states that ". . .no copyright shall subsist in the original text of any work which is in the public domain. . . ."

The concept of a specific public domain likewise was not a component of England's Statute of Anne, passed in 1710, after which the 1790 U.S. Copyright Act was closely patterned. In fact, the King's Bench in *Millar v. Taylor* 4 Burrow 2303, 98 Eng. Rep. 201 (K.B., 1769) held that common law copyright was perpetual and that a copyright *never fell into the public domain*. So to say the 1790 Act established the public domain is historically inaccurate. The concept of a public domain in relation to copyright law actually evolved later during the eighteenth century in the courts of England and France, where jurists described such concepts as *publici juris* and *propriété publique* in reference to works not covered by copyright. Thus, it should be apparent our modern focus on the sanctity and integrity of the public domain is not one of the apparent founding principles in the concept of copyright as envisioned by the Framers, and to use the phrase in the context of their thinking is, in my estimation, anachronistic.

So for sake of clarity, I will use the phrase "public domain" to refer only to creative works for which copyright protection does not exist for whatever reason. To help frame my issues, however, I will use the phrase "continuum of thought" or "continuum of knowledge" to refer to the early Romans concepts described above, *i.e.*, the basic building blocks of life and culture - data, facts, ideas, theories, and scientific principles - which are free for all to enjoy, combined with those works otherwise entitled to copyright protection that have fallen into the public domain. This distinction is critical to properly understand what our Forefathers intended to protect.

†††

To understand how our modern world has ostensibly affected the utilitarian underpinnings of copyright, it is important to segue for a moment into a more elaborate discussion about how Congress has use the authority granted to it by our Constitution. In order to maintain the aforementioned balance, Congress has established a copyright monopoly providing exclusive rights in tangible expressions of an idea. So it is, then, the proprietary nature of an original idea is based on *expression* of that idea in a manner that can be controlled, *i.e.*, a tangible format, again addressing the concern of Jefferson that an idea may be exclusively possessed as long as a person keeps it in their head, but "the moment it is divulged, it forces itself into the possession of everyone. . . every other possesses the whole of it." Specifically, in a famous passage of a letter written by Jefferson to McPherson, he described an idea as follows:

> He who receives an idea from me, receives instruction himself without lessening mine; as he who lights his taper at mine, receives light without darkening me. That ideas should freely spread from one to another over the globe, for the moral and mutual instruction of man and improvement of his condition, seems to have been peculiarly and benevolently designed by nature, when she made them, like fire, expansible over all space, without lessening their density at any point and like the air in which we breathe, move, and have our physical being, incapable of confinement or exclusive appropriation.

In other words, Jefferson is toying with the concept that an idea is more like energy than matter. The resulting corollary of this realization is that ideas themselves (energy), as well as the facts about the phenomena of the world, absent expression (matter), are considered to be the collective knowledge, or property, of humanity. Therefore, so far in history, what I have described as the ***continuum of knowledge*** has been made up of these unexpressed ideas together with the works that fell into the public domain. This is the tapestry of thought hanging over mankind from the beginning of time. The elements of the continuum of knowledge are distinct from the elements of the public domain, even though the two may contain overlapping items.

Although they certainly did not describe it as such, this continuum of knowledge was envisioned by our Forefathers to be for the greater good of society and is the reason, for example, an individual, tangible expressions of one of Claude Monet's favorite subjects, the Saint-George cathedral in Venice, theoretically entitled to copyright protection at the same time as the later paintings of François Salvat conveying expressions of the same subject. Once one of the painters' expressions of the idea that is the Saint George cathedral is transformed onto canvas, he is entitled to enforce the monopoly of copyright. Conversely, the mere idea or fact that is the cathedral itself is never the subject of individual property protection by the painter. But both the cathedral, the idea, and the painting, the expression, are part of the continuum of thought. Monet's expression of the idea may inspire me to write a novel about Venice or attempt to express my own unique and original ideas about the Saint- George cathedral through application of pigment to canvas.

The distinction is also codified in our current Copyright Act which states copyright law does not "protec[t]. . . any idea, procedure, process, system, method of operation, concept, principle, or discovery . . . described, explain, illustrated, or embodied in [the copyrighted] work" 107 United States Code §102(b). In *Eldred*, The Supreme Court recognized these elements, contained in a copyrighted work, are "instantly available for public exploitation at the moment of publication."

This is how copyright fuels the engine of free speech. Everyone is entitled to draw inspiration from the continuum of thought. This is why I say our Forefathers envisioned the societal benefit to start at the moment a work is circulated. At the moment of publication - not when the work falls into the public domain - the ideas expressed by the new work will inspire others to create their very own expressions of the same idea.

Stated another way, the law by necessity is focused on the *embodiment* of the idea, as opposed to the idea itself or, to use the biblical reference cited at the beginning of this chapter, it focuses on *the wine skins* more than the wine as a means of control. Embodiment, in this case, is equal to the expression. But this focus should not confuse our clarity about the distinct existence of the wine contained therein. It is the wine, after all, that we wish to protect - not the wineskin.

The U.S. Supreme Court described the concept of copyright as belonging to the "metaphysics of the law where the distinctions are . . . very subtle and refined and sometimes almost evanescent," perhaps echoing the thought of the English court in *Millar v. Taylor*. This conflation of the *expressed idea* - the "evanescent" - and the *physical embodiment* creates more misunderstanding regarding the concept of copyright than perhaps any other. In our advanced age of digitization - technological evanescence if you will - it is now more important than ever for us to remember the distinction between the two elements. At no time in prior history has the idea so closely resemble the expression of that idea flitting about as electrical impulses on the Internet.

The best illustration of this conflation is perhaps the area of musical works. For purposes of this discussion, we will ignore, for the moment, that there is a separate copyright for sound recordings, distinct from that in musical compositions. Our focus is primarily on the latter, *i.e.*, *the song*. In the late 1800's, popular songs were physically embodied sheet music sold by the publishers of Tin Pan Alley to patrons who would take them home and entertain their guest by playing them on the pianos in their parlor while they all sang. Then, in the early 1900's, radio replaced the parlor and vinyl records became the embodiment of choice for musical compositions, piped through the airways and played on what John Philip Sousa called "those inferno machines." This movement ultimately meant the end of Tin Pan Alley. The saga continued in the 60's, when it was the 8-track tape, and in the 70's, when it was the analog cassette. Finally, in the 80's, digital technology advanced and we began using the compact disc and digital audio tape. This ultimately led to the 90's and true digital format, the mp3 format, which leads us to the present. Once digitization became possible, all tangible expressions we subjected to the process and it became possible to make flawless copies of the "wine" that was paintings, photographs, text, music, graphics, video, sound recordings, and cartoons. In the words of the Supreme Court, we have reached the age of "evanescence." The wineskin is no longer a necessity.

John Perry Barlow, ex-Grateful Dead lyricist turned founder of the Electronic Frontier Foundation, describes this phenomenon:

Now, as information enters cyberspace . . . these [wine] bottles are vanishing. With the advent of digitization, it is now possible to replace all previous information storage forms with one metabottle: complex and highly liquid patterns of ones and zeros.

From the moment of digitization forward, the fusion of the expressed idea and the embodiment was "rent asunder," changing forever how we perceived copyright. Tangible expressions, once embodied in pigments, paper, strips of celluloid, discs of vinyl or plastic, and tape, now existed as glowing impulses of voltage conveyed in zeros and ones, flitting around the Internet at the speed of light. The expressions, in other words, are now closer to pure thought than our Forefathers perhaps ever dreamed possible. Digital technology thus threatens to disturb the delicate balance they intended to establish in their creation of a copyright monopoly. This truly *evanescent* nature of a *digital copyright monopoly* makes it extremely difficult to fit into the "old skin," *i.e.*, "an original idea expressed in a tangible format for more than transitory duration."

The "RAM Fixation" cases that arose in the late 90's - the seminal case being *MAI Systems Corp. v. Peak Computer*, 991 F.2d 511 (9th Cir. 1993, illustrate the difficulty precisely. In these cases, the courts struggled to determine whether a cached copy of a copyrighted work existing in the random access memory of a computer for no more than a second was sufficient "fixed in a tangible format" for more than a "transitory time," thus warranting protection under copyright law. The 9th Circuit in their *MAI Systems* case ruled that it was sufficient, but other courts, like the 2nd Circuit in *Cartoon Network v. CSC Holdings*, 536 F.3d 121 (2d Cir. 2008), found otherwise, ruling the copy was "fleeting" and therefore not "embodied . . . for a period of more than a transitory duration. . . ." The Supreme Court has yet to rule on this issue.

One thing is clear, however: once the veil was rent asunder, trying to enforce a copyright monopoly was somewhat akin to trying to sweep back the ocean with a broom. Trying to track down the digits as they shot across the Internet like stars across the Milky Way became an increasingly frustrating task for the music industry. Beginning with its efforts against Diamond Multimedia and its Rio Player in the late 90's (*Recording Indus. Ass'n of America, Inc. v. Diamond Multimedia Sys., Inc.*, 29 F. Supp.2d 624 (C.D. Cal. 1998), to its efforts against Napster (*A&M Records, Inc. v. Napster, Inc.*, 239 F.3d 1004 (2001) and Grokster (*MGM Studios, Inc. v. Grokster, Ltd.* 545 U.S. 913 (2005), and continuing through to the present with it efforts against more than 17,000 individual downloaders, the track record of the Record Industry Association of America in its fight against illegal downloading is the perfect example of this fruitless effort. The plight of the Motion Picture Association of America is not much better. Rather than adapt and transform our concepts of copyright - the wine skin - to conform to the new wine - digitization of art - the music and movie industries continue to cling to the status quo. Their hand was forced, in part, by decades of doing business under the old model in which the contracts were all based on the old containers.

What does this conundrum means for copyright law and the efficacy of a monopoly in the fruits of our creative labor? Before answering that question, and lest we forget, we will observe in the next chapter that new technologies have historically created challenges to Constitutional law. But while the implementation of the Copyright Clause may need to adapt to new technologies, new technologies have never been allowed to destroy the construct of the monopoly. The Constitutional jurisprudence has always adapted to conform to these new ideas and this presumes the copyright construct can, again, rise to the challenges of digitization it currently confronts. So, if we stand firm in our faith in the likes of Jefferson and Madison, we will view our founding document as a living, breathing document created to adapt to such challenges.

CHAPTER 2

Ideas that Spread Like Fire

*That ideas should freely spread from one to another over
the globe for the moral and mutual instruction of man,
and improvement of his condition, seems to have been
peculiarly and benevolently designed by nature,
when she made them, like fire, expansible over all space
without lessening their density in any point, and like the air in
which we breathe, move, and have our physical being,
incapable of confinement or exclusive appropriation.*

– Thomas Jefferson

It is safe to say none of the Framers of our Constitution knew the value of an original idea more than Thomas Jefferson. Jefferson was not only a politician, he was a great thinker; a scientist, inventor, architect, philosopher, educator, and epicurean. Jefferson invented the wheel cipher, hideaway bed, pedometer, swivel chair, dumbwaiter and, for those children in all of us, macaroni and cheese. He was the founder and chief architect for the University of Virginia and he served as both the first commissioner and examiner of the U.S. Patent Office, prior to his service as 2nd Vice President under John Adams and, obviously, as our 3rd President. It should be evident Jefferson knew the value of innovative thought.

Jefferson was uniquely qualified to inform us, as he did the delegates to the Constitutional Convention through his correspondence with them, about the fusion of ideas, intellectual property rights, invention, innovation, economic development, and democratic values. This is why his struggles with the idea of a government-granted monopoly in ideas and the ultimate acquiescence of his doubts about such grants are a poignant backdrop for our understanding of how to approach the conundrum created by digital technology.

The current digitization of creative arts and retail goods is not the first time in history a new technology has challenged an existing way of thinking. In the music industry, for example, the introduction of the "talking machine," a/k/a the phonorecord player, created such a stir John Philip Sousa testified before Congress the invention would "ruin the artistic development of music in this country" because our vocal chords would no longer be used and therefore vanish as a result of evolution. Very similar arguments are being made today in the context of digitization. What seems like an extreme position now is only perceived as such through the lenses of hindsight. The arguments being made against copyright today may seem as extreme to people in the future with the benefit of the same hindsight. Nonetheless, Congress responded to Sousa's and the industry's concerns, as it often does and is doing today, by revising the copyright law to address new technologies.

Concerns over advances in technology often inspire Congress to respond by creating legislation to address the new problems, which in turn stimulates the type of backlash we are seeing against copyright in our world today. To adequately address the issues when responding to the new technologies of any generation, we must keep returning to the primary objectives of Jefferson and others in the creation of copyright. The desire of these was to ensure the widespread distribution of ideas for the benefit of society by giving the creators of ideas a monopoly. As we observed earlier, the Founding Fathers were dedicated to encouraging the dissemination of mental creations throughout the New World where they could be used, entering the mind of others by assuring their creators they would be compensated for the value of such dissemination. Once certain limits were reached, the protected ideas would enter the public domain and become a part of the market place of ideas, freely available to the public for use in the creation of new ideas, although not owned by anyone.

This insertion of ideas into what I refer to as "the continuum of knowledge" or, for those Star Trek fans among us "the collective," occurs not only when the copyrighted work is inserted into the public domain, as some would argue, but *also, and more importantly,* when the work is originally created. To be sure, the latter insertion is what was envisioned by the Framers of our Constitution if they even had a concept of a public domain at all. The fact that the creator has to be compensated does not lessen the value to society envisioned by our great Leaders. This concept will be discussed in greater detail in later chapter.

Expressing what I believe is a similar thought, Jefferson believed widespread of dissemination of ideas "illuminated" the minds of society. In the preamble to his 1778 proposal for an educational system, aptly titled a "Bill for the More General Diffusion of Knowledge," Jefferson noted:

> . . . [E]ven under the best forms, those [governments] entrusted with power have, in time, and by slow operations, perverted it into tyranny; and it is believed that the most effectual means of preventing this would be, to illuminate, as far as practicable, the minds of the people at large . . . and [thereby] prompt [the people] to exert their natural powers to defeat its purpose.

This is the crux of Jefferson's philosophy: he believed this illumination of minds, *i.e.*, widespread dissemination of ideas into the continuum of knowledge, was an essential safeguard against tyranny. In the end, it directly informed his view of the value of the copyright monopoly. Jefferson believed drawing on that continuum of existing knowledge to invent and innovate was necessary for the economic development of a growing nation. In a subsequent writing dated 1821, Jefferson elaborates on this aspect:

> . . . in an infant country like ours we must depend for improvement on science of other countries, longer established, possessing better means, and more advanced than we are. To prohibit us from the benefit of a foreign light is to consign us to darkness.

These are words the United States would have been wise to heed during the more than 100 years from 1886 to 1989 while it refused to sign the Berne Convention for the worldwide protection of literary and artistic works. The Supreme Court wisely understood the principle Jefferson explained, *i.e.*, that prohibiting foreign works consigns us to darkness, in their recent opinion in *Golan v. Holder* in which they upheld the Constitutionality of the legislation implementing Article 18 of the Berne treaty.

In 1787, Jefferson extolled the value of Jeudy de l'Hommande's invention of a methodology that improved the preservation of flour, writing that "[e]very discovery which multiplies the subsistence of men, must be a matter of joy to every friend of humanity." Jefferson's accolade to de l'Hommande can be understood as an subset of the same principle expressed by John Donne in Meditation XVII:

No man is an island, entire of itself; every man is a piece of the continent, a part of the main. If a clod be washed away by the sea, Europe is the less . . .: any man's death diminishes me, because I am involved in mankind, and therefore never send to know for whom the bells tolls; it tolls for thee.

Just as mankind or, to use Locke's terminology, "society" suffers as a result of one individual death, so too does society benefit from the creation of an individual expression. Jefferson ultimately grew to be the most fervent proponent of encouraging an individual's contribution to the continuum of thought by offering the incentive of the monopoly in that expression.

The problem with many solutions being proposed by advocates of copyright today, as well as those who would have us do away with the concept entirely, is that they do not emphasize the delicate balance discussed in the prior chapter, but rather focus on only one aspect of the continuum of knowledge principal while ignoring the other. The expressed idea is just as confined when embodied in electrical impulses as it was when it was embodied in physical materials. Just because we can now "unclothe" the idea by stripping away its tangible, physical embodiment, does not eliminate the system of confinement, *i.e. the copyright monopoly*, envisioned by the Forefathers. The need for their construct of copyright is as real today as it was in the 1700s. Just as we need self-made borders to protect the legal construct that we call *real property*, so too do we need the borders of copyright law to define what we protect as *intellectual property*. The wine need not be spilled just because the borders, in this analogy the wineskin, are more difficult for us to perceive.

As can be seen in the quote at the head of this chapter, Jefferson grabbled with the concept that an idea was "incapable of confinement" even as the original Copyright Clause was being debated and drafted. He nevertheless clearly chose to participate in and support the creation of a system that would, in fact, confine that very thing he said was incapable of confinement. He recognized that while an invention was not capable of confinement in nature, such confinement was possible by fiat through a creation of law. So, even though the creations of authors and inventors, now more than ever, more closely resemble a mere idea, using the legal tools given to us by our Forefathers, our society can still adapt our system to offer incentives to authors and inventors for the dissemination of the fruits of their labors.

Through new technologies and interpretations, we have developed *virtual bottles* to store our new wine, bottles which replaced the old physical, less evanescent *wine skins of embodiment*. Our current copyright constructs have molded themselves to adapt to evolving technologies. This phenomenon is what I call the *cognitive dispensation*, a concept I explore in the next chapter. But first, as a summary of my exploration of Jefferson's resolution about confinement of ideas, even digital expressions of an idea can be perceived through the use of various electronic devices and, as such, are confined. In the final analysis of this issue, it is important to remember our laws are meant to reflect public opinion: as Jefferson explained, "...governments are republican only in proportion as they embody the will of their people, and execute it." Perhaps in the end, the future of the copyright monopoly may depend more on society's perceptions than it does on the government's restrictive regulations. In the end, it is my goal to illustrate to the reader that Jefferson's views about intellectual property reflect our current society's perceptions more accurately than most people realize and, by doing so, convince him or her society has a responsibility to support the concept of a copyright monopoly.

CHAPTER 3

The Cognitive Dispensation

Suppose now that there were two such magic rings [of invisibility], and the just [person] put on one of them and the unjust the other; no man can be imagined to be of such an iron nature that he would stand fast in justice. No man would keep his hands off what was not his own when he could safely take what he liked out of the market . . . and in all respects be like a God among men. Then the actions of the just would be as the actions of the unjust; they would both come at last to the same point.

And this we may truly affirm to be a great proof that a man is just, not willingly or because he thinks that justice is any good to him individually, but of necessity, for wherever any one thinks that he can safely be unjust, there he is unjust. For all men believe in their hearts that injustice is far more profitable to the individual than justice. . . .

If you could imagine any one obtaining this power of becoming invisible, and never doing any wrong or touching what was another's, he would be thought by the lookers-on to be a most wretched idiot, although they would praise him to one another's faces, and keep up appearances with one another from a fear that they too might suffer injustice.

Plato's' *The Republic*, Book II

One perceived effect of digital technologies is that the elimination of the tangible embodiment of the expression somehow gives the "power" or "control" back to the people and this shift in control eliminates any obligation to comply with social mores and codes. More to the point, there is a prevailing sense in the power of the Internet to shield a person's identity in such a way they will not "get caught" downloading a pirated movie. In a very real and modern sense, the Internet is the equivalent of Gyges' magical ring of invisibility, developed in the second book of Plato's classic work, The Republic. In the story as told by Glaucon to his teacher, Socrates, Gyges is a shepherd who finds a magical ring in a chasm created by a lightning storm. Mysteriously, the ring gives him a cloak of invisibility. Using his newfound magical power, Gyges seduces the Queen of Lydia and murders the King. He then takes over the throne and gains enormous power, wealth and fame. Glaucon's point is there is no justice, but rather it is power that controls what is right and what is wrong. In other words, "might makes right."

In the above quotation, Glaucon argues that given a similar opportunity, any person, whether they were just or unjust, would use the power of their invisibility to commit as many crimes as necessary to get whatever they want, without any fear of retribution [Book II, 359d]. Glaucon was responding to Socrates' refutation of similar arguments put forth by Thrasymachus in Book I of The Republic, i.e., that "justice is nothing but the advantage of the stronger" [Book I, 338c].

So, you might justifiably ask, how does this ancient diatribe relate to the issue of Copyright law in the 21st Century? To understand the relation, consider a study on counterfeiting activity over the Internet conducted by a company called Envisional at the expense and request of NBC Universal. The results of this study are literally astonishing: 24% of all global Internet traffic involves digital theft of some form! Stated another way, 1 in every 4 people surfing the Internet are stealing intellectual property, i.e., illegally downloading either copyrighted or trademarked materials. According to the International Federation of the Phonographic Industry, 95% of the music downloaded from the Internet is downloaded illegally. Now consider whether these same people who so quickly download a song or a movie on the Internet without paying for it would also walk up to an artist selling their painting in the park and steal one of their paintings. I firmly believe the answer to the latter question is a resounding no. But why? What is different about the World Wide Web, *i.e.* cyberspace, that gives these consumers the feeling they are entitled to download music and movies through mechanisms like BitTorrent or The Pirate Bay without compensating those who created such product? What are these people thinking? I think the answer can be found in the writings of Plato cited above.

Imagine now that instead of downloading intangible digital copies of sound recordings and musical compositions, one out of every four people in retail malls were carrying out stolen *tangible* merchandise on a daily basis, or if 95% of the product leaving the mall was stolen. The general populace would consider that to be total chaos, even anarchy, yet they do not respond the same way when songwriters suffer the same fate at the hands of online thievery. Why?

Glaucon's experiment in thought informs us both as to why society does not react in the same way and even more precisely, why a person who would not normally steal a *tangible* object in the physical world is nonetheless more than willing to download music or movies, *i.e.*, *intangible objects*, on the Internet for free: because the fear of being punished or getting caught is greatly diminished in the evanescent world of Cyberspace. The Internet, like Gyge's magical ring, confers upon its users an ostensible cloak of invisibility.

As one astute commentator surmised in response to an interview with Alice in Chain's lead singer, Sean Kinney, "The real reason people steal music is that they CAN and very easily." That this is a truth is evident from the plethora of how to guides on the Internet, teaching people "how not to get caught" using BitTorrent sites to download infringing expressions. Any argument to the contrary is mere justification for actions people who otherwise know in their hearts are wrong. But more on that later.

It's important to read Socrates' response to his student, as told by the sophistry of Plato, to understand the relevance of *The Republic* fully, for in it Glaucon's viewpoint is portrayed by Plato as false. His argument in the remaining portion of *The Republic* is the just man *would not* be tempted by this cloak of invisibility bestowed upon him by this magical ring in order to validate the commission of unjust acts. Rather, Socrates says in character, the just man understands crime, *i.e.*, *injustice*, in and of itself makes a person unhappy. The just man understands, in other words, he is better off to remain just. Stated another way, a just man acts according to his nature, *i.e.*, his own natural law.

I frequently discuss this issue with undergraduate students when teaching courses on copyright and cyberspace law. One of my students made the following observation, which reinforces the conclusions drawn by Socrates. She said:

> I do not follow the rules because I am scared of [being busted] for illegal downloading. I follow the rules because I have respect for the people who wrote and

recorded the songs, and even more, because I want to work in the music industry.

So, this student's actions are not affected by the cloak of invisibility offered by the Internet. Like the proverbial "just man" of Socrates, she believes she is better off being true to her nature.

Another relevant opinion is offered in the excellent blog article found on arbiteronline.com titled *Illegal downloading: The real cost of 'free' music.* In that article, a student at Boise State discussing the same issue is quoted as saying:

> I don't do it because I don't feel it's right. If I were making the music, I'd be upset if people were downloading it for free.

For these two students, following the rules is not about whether or not they'll be caught; it's about doing the right thing. More precisely, these students are motivated by their own nature, by their sense of fairness and justice. Further, for both of these students, the emphasis in on honoring, *i.e. compensating,* the people who created the music. This illustrates Plato's point precisely: a just person understands that even with a cloak of invisibility, doing the right thing makes a person happy or, in the words of the Boise student, makes the person "feel right."

The Internet is also very much the Land of Oz. By that analogy I mean in addition to this cloak of invisibility endowed to us by the Internet, the technology also deceives us with illusions of anonymity. Like the Wizard in the Land of Oz, hiding behind the curtain, it is not so much that the user is anonymous -

merely another form of invisibility - but rather it is difficult to know the identity of the *person behind the curtain.* For our purposes, that is the creator of the music or movie being downloaded. As Trent Reznor, the famous lead singer of Nine Inch Nails, illustrated in an interview, "there is a perception that you don't pay for music when [you download it or when] your hear it . . . on MySpace."

Because of its sheer vastness and mysteriousness, Cyberspace gives people false perceptions that their actions on the Internet do not affect the real people in the non-virtual world, or in my analogy, the people behind the curtain. This, coupled with the cloak of invisibility, creates an illusion that "resistance is futile": everyone is doing it, so I can too. No one will get caught. It's not affecting anyone but the record label conglomerates and the greedy movie producers and media giants.

Cyberspace alters our reality in that it makes the real people behind the music and movies an amorphous, anonymous entity. Because the average Internet surfer doesn't see the people who spent hours writing the words and crafting the music, molding them into a well-refined song, they are not aware when they download a digital recording of that song for free, the songwriters do not get paid, whereas when a physical copy of that song is sold, they do. This scenario does not even take into account the work of the producer, engineer, studio musicians, or even the artist involved in the recording, all of whom also suffer a loss of revenue from the activity. All of these people are deprived of income as a result of a free digital download. The fact opponents of restricting such piracy characterize these very real people as a corporate conglomerate does not alter this deprivation, but rather is the crux of the misunderstanding. The attitude results in a simplistic and ill-placed justification: it is much easier to steal from an amorphous, anonymous entity or better yet, a corporate evil than it is to steal from a struggling songwriter, or poor artist, particularly when all your friends are doing it. Like the Wizard of Oz, it was easier for the Tin Man to criticize and condemn the man behind the curtain whose identity was unknown to him when, in reality, it was the Wizard who gave him his heart in the end.

So most people who are illegally downloading music from the Internet have no idea who they are affecting or how widespread the effect is. They do not understand that it is the creator who gives them the very thing they enjoy. For example, most of these same people would not even think about walking up on stage after a singer/songwriter performing in a nightclub takes a break and stealing his guitar. Yet that very same person likely doesn't give much thought to taking the singer/songwriter's song - his intellectual work - from the Internet.

Likewise, the thought of stealing the filmmaker's camera would be physically abhorrent to most people, but to those 1 in 4 people who are downloading the latest Hollywood release for free, it doesn't faze their consciousness one iota. It is easy to steal from the amorphous mass of anonymity behind the veil of the Internet, but that simplicity doesn't make it right.

Some opponents of intellectual property laws who have contributed to the ongoing dialog argue that these two thefts are not analogous, *i.e.*, that theft of stealing a physical object versus taking a digital object. The former deprives the owner of the physical object, the argument goes, while the latter is merely making another digital copy and does not deprive the owner of the original. This argument confuses what Plato called "the temporal dispensation" with what I've described as the "cognitive dispensation." By that, I mean we've entered a dispensation in which our original thought is no longer tied to the temporal, physical world through tangible expression, but rather is tied to what may best be described as the "cognitive," the mere electronic impulses currently embodying thought. These impulses are still an expression fixed and perceivable, but the expression can be deconstructed, rerouted across numerous networks, and reassembled in an instant, thereby resembling the cognitive functions of our brain much more precisely than any physical embodiment could. I discuss this in much more detail in a later chapter, so suffice it to say here I believe the two thefts to be equivocal and this phenomenon of the cognitive dispensation does not negate the fact.

The equivocation is also illustrated by recent efforts by a website called "redigi.com" to sell "used" digital copies of MP3 files pursuant to the Copyright Act's "first sale doctrine." The first sale doctrine allows a person who purchases the physical embodiment of a copyright to resell that physical embodiment. This means when I purchase a physical CD recording of a musical composition, the creator of the composition cannot restrict me from reselling the physical CD to a used CD shop. Redigi argues the resale of a digital copy is the same as the resale of a physical copy. How this situation plays out in litigation is yet to be seen, but it nonetheless illustrates the conundrums present in the cognitive dispensation.

Finally, a recent analysis conducted by the Institute for Policy Innovation tends to support my equivocation of the theft of physical and digital objects as well. The report also disproves the idea that copying a digital file does not deprive the owner of anything, as does physical theft. The report indicated music piracy causes $12.5 billion in economic losses every year. It further concluded 71,060 U.S. jobs are lost, with a total loss of $2.7 billion in workers' earnings. Such reports abound throughout the industry, yet many of the people guilty of illegal downloading continue to view these reports as industry-driven and, therefore, skewed. A recent comment by frequent anti-copyright blogger Michael Arrington serves as a very timely illustration of this distrust of the evidence:

> Eventually the reality of the Internet will force the laws to change, too. One way or another the music labels will eventually surrender, and recorded music will be free. Until it is, I refuse to feel guilty for downloading and sharing music. Every time I listen to a song, or share it with a friend, I'm doing the labels a favor. One that eventually I should be paid for. [sic] Until that day comes, don't even think about trying to tell me that I'm doing something ethically wrong when it's considered quite legal, with the labels' blessing, in China.

To be blunt, Arrington ignores clear evidence. Such defiant opinions as those expressed here by Mr. Arrington miss the fact conveyed earlier that very real people – *not amorphous masses or giant conglomerates* – are being affected; furthermore, the effect on them is actually devastating. This tactic is common among antagonists of the copyright monopoly, who often describe the owners of copyright as "the content industry" or "media conglomerates," redirecting the attention away from the individual creator and on to the faceless corporations. Sometimes, as in the film titled *RIP, A Remix Manifesto* by Brent Gaylor, these corporations are called out by name, usually with the focus being on the multimedia giant, the Disney Corporation.

But it the real world, individual creative souls are the ones who suffer the most as a direct effect of callous attitudes and sophistry like Arrington's & his ilk. These creative souls, like me, shudder at the prediction that someday "recorded music will be free." Today it is MP3 music files, tomorrow it will be manufactured products and, in the future, who knows, maybe our DNA coding will be available to download; all for free.

As an entertainment attorney, many of my clients are creative people. Many are the real people who are being injured by these biased attitudes of copyright antagonists. I have many songwriter clients who no longer create their art because they are forced to take odd jobs to support their families. The performance royalties they used to receive from performance rights organizations such as ASCAP, BMI or SESAC are down by half or more from a just few years ago. Their mechanical royalty checks from use of their musical compositions on sound recordings are virtually non-existent, because no one buys physical product anymore. These songwriters simply cannot afford to create simply for the sake of creation, as they work multiple jobs to support themselves and their families. Even if they do create for the mere sake of creation itself, they are not as prolific as they were when they were paid to do it. These songwriters simply don't have the time to create art for which they receive no compensation. They are living examples of the fact that taking away the incentive to create deprives society of their creations and chokes the continuum of thought. The simple fact is if the "fruits of our labor" go unrewarded, we tend to find other labor to support our basic needs. In short, we are regressing to pre-1790 status in America and, once again, need to heed the advice of Jefferson and Madison: our society needs to provide incentives to its authors and inventors in order to encourage the creation of art and inventions.

This same regression is happening to my non-songwriting clients in other artistic industries: literature, classic paintings, photography, and film making. Nothing escapes the breadth of digitization. Now, with the burgeoning technology of "3-D printing," even sculptural arts, manufactured merchandise, and other forms of physical "widgets" can no longer escape massive unchecked duplication through digitization. The actual diminishing of the creation of arts argues strongly against the assertions of Boldrin & Levine, cited earlier, who claim they have produced examples of "frenetic creation in the absence of copyright." Boldrin & Levine, with all due respect, are obviously not engaged in the creative community. What will become of the arts if Messrs. Boldrin, Levine, Arrington, and Gaylor among others, have their way and intellectual property laws are eliminated? Will creators continue to create? Will inventors continue to invent? Do these antagonists expect all the creative arts will be available for duplication for free? Do they expect all merchandise will be available to "print" for free? Is that what we want as a society? I suggest we carefully consider the alternatives before we answer that question, as it is in direct conflict with the incentive system our Forefathers invented on our behalf over 200 years ago.

In as simple a way as I can say it, our Forefathers believed without incentive, inventors and artists would not invent and create. In other words, our artistic and inventive community will suffer from the same consequence as my songwriting clients, forced to get jobs to support their livelihood, their opportunity for creation will diminish. We will be left with hobbyists who create what they can muster the energy in their spare time.

This diversion into my cognitive dispensation theory brings us full circle to Plato and the Ring of Gyges: in answer to Glaucon, Socrates postulated the root of all trouble, or injustice, is *unlimited desire.* How apropos is that in response to the attitude conveyed by Mr. Arrington? How applicable is that to this post-digitized world of Cyberspace, this world of rampant illegal downloading? For the music industry, which ultimately led the charge against piracy, it all started when the Recording Industry Association of America sued Diamond Multimedia for their introduction of the RIO MP3 player, which brought the concept of digitized music into society's field of view. After that, Shawn Fanning produced the popular Napster software, that exploded society's awareness. Almost everyone found every song they ever loved available on Napster, for free. It's as if they were Harrison Ford discovering the treasure room in an unknown, ancient tomb: everything your heart desires is within your grasp. It's yours for the taking.

With its cloak of invisibility and its illusion of anonymity, what the Internet did, in short, was return the power, as it were, back to the people. This is where we started in this chapter: the Internet gives people the means to fulfill their unfulfilled desires. Now, everyone can be a creator, a publisher, and a distributor. No one needs the traditional industry conglomerates anymore — the people have all access. They fulfilled their unlimited desire. And, as Mr. Arrington points out, they don't even feel a tinge of quilt. Or do they?

I am encouraged by the words of the two intelligent students from Belmont University and Boise quoted earlier who, despite the tidal wave of opposition to original expression, still possess a strong sense of justice. As Lord Acton said, we should beware: "Power tends to corrupt, and absolute power corrupts absolutely." Lord Acton is implying that with power comes responsibility. These two students accept that responsibility, but for every one of those who do, there are statistically three who reject it. Unfortunately for the creative industries, the power is currently being abused and will, ultimately, mean the end of the industry as it existed through the 20th century unless the creators regain that power. Mr. Arrington's world of free arts will be a reality if we do not come to the realization our Forefathers did hundreds of years ago - having a *monopoly* on an idea *for a limited time* motivates creators to create - we will find ourselves without the exploitation of *new ideas*. Original thought will diminish and likely perish.

So what does this mean for those of us who have chosen to make our living in the world of creation? Does it mean the end of our industry? Do we, as Mr. Arrington would suggest, have to resort to giving away our creative endeavors for free? Does it mean an end to copyright law as it exists?

Many opponents, led by the likes of John Perry Barlow of the Electronic Frontier Foundation and Dr. Lawrence Lessig of Creative Commons, say just that: our current system of copyright protection is fatally flawed and cannot be repaired through legislative amendments. Recall the quote from Barlow discussed in an earlier chapter: in a stroke of understated arrogance and borrowing from the Gospel of Mark without attribution, he claims we are trying to put "new wine" into "old wine skins." Never mind that, as a lyricist for the Grateful Dead, Barlow's soap box upon which he proclaims this "wisdom" was built on the shoulders of the very copyright system he condemns.

Lessig, on the other hand, takes a rather *laissez faire*, almost submissive approach. He maintains the creative industry's piracy problems cannot be stopped so, he says, we should just throw our hands up and ignore all the infringement. Specifically, Lessig argues the infringing activity is merely a form of cultural expression in the form of remix and as such, should simply be ignored so as not to criminalize those cultures reusing original creative expressions in order to create derivative works. Lessig's proposed model of "creative commons" licensing is intended as a solution to give those who want to donate their expressions to these cultures the ability to allow their works to be used freely with only attribution.

Just as Barlow's pulpit is built using his profits from the creative industry, Lessig's creative commons is built on the framework of the existing copyright system as well. So, in a very real sense, the critics of U.S. copyright law, despite describing themselves as the "copyLeft" are, to a great degree, simply building on the existing structure which they critique.

A review of other scholarly treatises reveals a litany of reforms designed to address the perceived problems. For example, in an article appearing in the Iowa Law Review, *Real Copyright Reform*, Janet Litman proposed that personal, non-commercial usages be exempt from regulation under the copyright law, so as to focus the law solely on *commercial* usages.

This is no different from Lessig's "hands up" approach. It doesn't solve the problem, it merely ignores it in an exasperated fashion.

It is not surprising to me opponents build their arguments on the back of copyright concepts, as this is what our Forefathers, particularly Thomas Jefferson, foresaw when they conceived the monopoly of copyright. If we examine its origins— *i.e., the protection of an original idea expressed in a tangible way* – the concept of copyright protection passed down to us from our Forefathers is a concept allowing society to build on ideas of the past, not only once those ideas pass out of the creator's monopoly and into the public domain, *but after they have been published and are available to the public for consumption.* As a society, we too follow their example and build into our system of protection a means by which creators can still profit from their unique ideas, but allow free speech and the marketplace of ideas to flourish. Recently, the Supreme Court recognized that once an expression of an idea is disseminated, the ideas embedded therein can be freely used to inspire new expressions.

To succeed, any proposals for reform of copyright must conform to the ideology of our U.S. heritage. Drawing distinctions such as those drawn by Litman between commercial and non-commercial use do little to reflect the spirit of copyright and, in fact, eradicate the intent of our Forefathers. Regardless of its commerciality, when the misuse of a copyright decreases the creators' incentive to create and distribute new works, this conflicts with the intent of the Constitution. Lessig's Creative Common licensing structure at least does more to promote the dissemination of creative works, but at the same time it provides adequate incentives and, therefore, also ignores the principles established by our Founding Fathers when they created the Constitution.

When scholars and professors propose such radical reforms as these, they are fueling the antagonists of copyright and essentially siding with the likes of Arrington, who would have us do away with copyright laws in order to expand their collection of music for free. If we find substantial reform of copyright laws is necessary, such a reform should not be dictated by the whims of digital thieves nor developed in reaction to a feelings of helpless despair. Rather, as all laws, any proposed reform should reflect a reasoned accounting of what is best for society as a whole without the decay of individual rights. If law indeed reflects the people's desires, this raises the question of what does society want its copyright laws to achieve?

One potential answer to that question can be found by examining the now famous Radiohead experiment in which Trent Reznor and crew allowed consumers to pay what they wanted and only if they wanted to, for the latest release of Nine Inch Nails, it turned out 18% of the consumers chose to do so. That, to me, is an encouraging statistic and one that confirms a belief in the economic benefits of creating art. Nearly one in five people, *even with the cloak of anonymity provided by the Ring of Gyges of this era, i.e., Cyberspace,* chose to pay the creators for their creation. Take that Glaucon! Take that Arrington!

So what does that tell us about society's desires? At the very least, it says almost one in five people will chose to do the *just thing*, as Plato predicted, even when the tide of conformity rises above their heads and their friends encourage them to take what they want under the cloak of invisibility. It seems the intuitive wisdom of Plato is correct after all. It also seems that perhaps our Founding Fathers may have had the right idea.

Moreover, and hopefully without donning my theological background and stepping into the pulpit, this statistic proves a significant portion of our society still understands the benefits of living a just life. The bottom line is it really doesn't matter what laws are passed by society, there will always be a certain percentage of people who will chose to steal, take and plunder, whether it be because they are more powerful or because they are cloaked with invisibility or shielded by anonymity. But – and here is the important point – there will also always be a segment of society who recognize the idea Thomas Hobbes first advanced hundreds of years ago, *i.e.*, the utilitarian idea of "giving to every man his own." If a man bakes a loaf of bread, is it not his right to trade that to the artist for whose painting he wishes to barter?

Hobbes' idea was later developed by the likes of John Stuart Mill, which trickled down through Locke into the philosophy of our Forefathers and was incorporated into their drafts of Article I, Section 8, Clause 8 of the U.S. Constitution. As we know, this gives Congress the authority "[to] promote the progress of science and useful arts, by securing for limited times to Authors and Inventors the exclusive rights to their respective Writings and Discoveries."

Without this Constitutional right, a creator has no hope of protecting his or her property against plunder. And as long as a segment of society believes this proposition to be beneficial to society as a whole, it will hopefully continue to motivate creators to create, and so profit from their creations just as our

Forefathers intended, despite the efforts of those who choose to destroy it under a cloak of invisibility - Arrington said "I refuse to feel guilty for downloading and sharing music" – and, like Gyges, unjustly take for themselves the kingdom of Lydia. But if we are finally to ward off the Gyges of the world who would destroy the kingdom of copyright, we need a thorough understanding of the philosophical underpinnings involving both property and monopoly. For that, we need to understand the philosophies and thoughts that fired the synapses in the minds of Thomas Jefferson and James Madison.

CHAPTER 4

The Philosophical Underpinnings of Copyright

All wealth is the product of labor.

-John Locke

Property must be secured or liberty cannot exist.

-John Adams

When they began to draw the outlines of a new nation, the Framers of our Constitution were working from a blank slate, and so crafted each concept and each provision very carefully. Much of their thinking was guided by the early leaders of our new country. Of all of these leaders, Jefferson, in particular, grabbled with the potential dichotomy of giving a tangible monopoly to an intangible idea, and thereby abridging the ideas of others. His machinations of thought were lubricated by the surrounding philosophies of the day. The same could be said for James Madison and Charles Pinckney, who ultimately fashioned the Copyright Clause. All of the Framers of our Constitution were influenced by the trend in thought of the day. It will benefit our understanding of our current copyright construct, therefore, if we explore the philosophies that framed their reference point.

Our Forefathers were avid readers, particularly in the philosophical and political thoughts of the day. They were intellectual giants, fluent in writings spanning many centuries, including such notables as Plato, Cicero, John Locke, Montesquieu, David Hume, Isaac Newton, Sir William Blackstone, John Milton, just to name a few. But in one journal article examining the subject, Professor Forrest McDonald says in order to understand the mind of our Founding Fathers, the writings these great men studied have to be understood in the context of what they had been through, as is true for any person. According to McDonald, this combination of experience and knowledge gave our early leaders. . .

> a broad intellectual matrix, a set of related frames of reference, through which certain of the obstacles to the erection of viable free institutions became visible. What they read, when tempered by hard experience, enabled the Fathers to understand that the road to freedom is not toll-free, and to point out some of the pitfalls along the path. One could hardly ask for a more precious lesson.

The experience of the late 1700s "tempered" our Forefathers studies about government, liberty, and property and gave them perspective, says McDonald. Events such as the Declaration of Independence, the American Revolution, and the election of our first President, all served to inform and influence the creation of the laws governing this new land, the Constitution in particular.

Through the sieve of their experiences, the Framers perceived a government too small was just as dangerous as a government that was too intrusive. They grew to understand that the needs of society had to take precedent over the needs of the individuals, yet the individual had to be guaranteed certain rights. Our Forefathers quickly learned that without a balanced government having the power to enforce personal liberties, neither liberty nor property were safe. It is critical to remember the concept of intellectual properties and monopolies in those properties, arose as part of these considerations. In short, the Framers had to create a type of government never in existence before in history. To do so, our Founding Fathers turned to philosophies to date to derive their inspiration.

With specific regard to original ideas, the first system of patent registration was developed in 1790, shortly after the Constitutional Convention, and the same year the first copyright act was passed. The influence of the surrounding culture cannot be diminished: our Forefathers' thinking regarding intellectual property was heavily impacted by the current thought and experiences of the moment. Much of their thinking regarding intellectual property circled around the somewhat disparate concepts of John Locke's "natural philosophy" and "consequentialism" or "utilitarianism" heavily influenced by the writings of John Stuart Mill and Jeremy Bentham.

Utilitarianism can be characterized, quoting Bentham, as "the greatest happiness principle," *i.e.*, it demands that the correct actions are the one that will bring the greatest amount of happiness to the greatest number of people in a given society. While utilitarianism may be considered a form of naturalism, pure "natural rights" philosophy maintains that the rules governing society should be dictated by the universe, *i.e.*, "universal" or "natural" laws. During the Enlightenment, John

Locke was considered the premiere advocate of natural rights as they apply to governing, as expressed in his *An Essay Concerning Human Understanding*, and his *Second Treatise on Civil Government*.

John Locke's philosophy, particularly the *Second Treatise on Civil Government*, spoke loudly to the hearts of Americans on the eve of Independence as they faced the formation of a new government, a *Tabula Rasa*, or "blank slate." Madison, who had the most direct influence on our current copyright construct, described Locke's *Second Treatise* as a work "admirably calculated to impress on young minds the right of nations to establish their own governments and to inspire a love of free ones."

Inherent in the philosophy and writings of Locke was the idea that people are basically "naturally" good, as its namesake implies. Locke taught that man was born with a "tabula rasa," *i.e.*, they were blank, with the propensity for *neither* good nor evil. Instead, he believed in the Romantic concept that man had "boundless virtue" and was born with limitless possibilities: what you write upon your blank pad is up to you.

Drawing on these basic theories of natural law, Locke developed his concept of "natural liberty" intended to place limitations on governmental, or civil, authority. In this construct, if people are good and, as Locke believed, government is evil, the more people are involved in their government - *i.e.*, the more democratic the government, the better government would be.

In Locke's theory of natural liberty, then, government arises from "inconveniences" in the state of human nature and, as such, is based on human need. Locke thus placed the locus of a government's authority in the hands of a voluntary contract among all people to enter into a civil society, *i.e.*, what Hobbes called the "social contract." Locke's concept of the social contract differed from that of Hobbes, however, in that the sovereignty of the people is not *permanently* transferred to an absolute "sovereign," but is only temporarily delegated to a government of limited power.

Locke's arguments against an arbitrary and autocratic government structure had a profound and permanent influence on political thought in general, but most certainly had a tremendous impact on the thinking of our Founding Fathers. In addition to the influence of Locke, however, our Forefathers had history and theory on their side and as McDonald pointed out, tempered these ivory tower philosophies with real world experience.

The Framers realized that, in practice, democratic governments required the assent of all people historically possessed an inevitable appetite for power and, therefore, eventually degenerated into tyranny. In their view, pure democracy tended to be antithetical to liberty.

To counteract this potential degeneration, our Founding Fathers inserted property rights as a wall between the government and personal liberty, borrowing from the part of Locke's philosophy which taught property rights were a part of natural laws, existing prior to the establishment of any government system. For Locke, legitimate government was contractual: the people to be governed would agree to support the government so long as it, in turn, supported their inherent rights of property, including their rights to liberty.

Property rights, then, according to Locke and our Founding Fathers, provide economic independence. This independence empowers individuals and gives them the power to participate in the political process, thereby challenging government policy. This places limits on the reach of government. Supreme Court Justice Joseph Story, author of the *Commentaries on the Constitution of the United States*, once opined, "The fundamental maximums of a free government seem to require that the rights of personal liberty and private property should be held sacred." By extension, Justice Story's emphasis on the importance of private property in the framework of a free government includes an equally important emphasis on a sacrosanct intellectual property.

But before connecting the philosophical dots between property, intellectual property, and the current copyright construct, we must also examine the teachings of another influential thinking of the Enlightenment, Jeremy Bentham. Bentham, the father of utilitarianism, disagreed with the foundational principle of natural law found in Locke's theories, calling the idea of natural rights "nonsense on stilts." In *A Fragment of Government*, written in 1776, Bentham wrote that the fundamental principle of his philosophy was that the true measure of what was right or wrong was not any "natural law," but rather that which brought "the greatest happiness of the greatest number [of people]." As applied to government, then, he believed a legitimate government would measure the pains and pleasures associated with any proposed legislation and create laws that would achieve the greatest good for the greatest number of people. Instead of a covenant with the people, then, he believed governments arise by habit or by force. In order for a contract to be binding, the government must already exist in order to enforce it.

Bentham also is credited with the concept of the "free market," a principle heavily influencing our economic policies to this day. In his book, *Defense of Usury*, as an example, he argues interest rates should be free from governmental control. This principle is borne out in the U.S. Federal Reserve System which, although authorized by acts of Congress, is "independent" from government in that "its monetary policy decisions do not have to be approved by the President or anyone else in the executive or legislative branches of government." His concept of a free market system would later inform the thinking of Jefferson and Madison as they tried to conceive of a system of incentives for encouraging a "free marketplace of ideas."

Although Bentham was not very well known during his lifetime, many of Bentham's teachings would ultimately find their way into the mainstream of American thinking through the writings of his student, John Stuart Mill, and those of his friend, Adam Smith, with whom he corresponded frequently. Smith, as history has shown, expanded on Bentham's concept of a free market, giving the U.S. the underpinnings of its current economic system. He wrote that a free market is a market without economic intervention and regulation by government. For Smith, the only exception to this prohibition against governmental regulation was government may regulate to the degree necessary to enforce ownership of property rights and contractual obligations.

Smith also believed an economy should be free of monopolies in which any entity, including the individual, persistently gains a greater market share than can be achieved through competition. The free market economic system as conceived by Smith, therefore, disfavors any monopoly, especially those instituted at the hand of government, unless there is a significantly compelling justification. Smith's disdain for governmental monopolies, absent adequate justification, made its way into the minds of our Founding Fathers, especially the minds of Jefferson and Madison.

The writings of our Forefathers illustrate both an understanding and appreciation of Bentham's and Locke's philosophy. This is most evident in Jefferson's conclusion that "Inventions . . . cannot, *in nature*, be a subject of property." The modifying phrase "in nature" was a red flag to McPherson, the recipient of this particular letter, that Jefferson meant his discussion to be taken in the context of utilitarianism, not natural rights. In order to properly understand the point Jefferson is trying to make, then, it is necessary to understand his words in the context of utilitarian thought, something which modern readers often overlook in their interpretations.

However, since Bentham was the author of the British government's "unofficial" response to the Declaration of Independence, criticizing and mocking many of its principles, we can assume he was not the favorite of most of the Founding Fathers. So, despite Jefferson's leanings, the cultural Zeitgeist of early America would have naturally tended to favor Locke over Bentham and so we see traces of natural law in our copyright law in addition to its overriding utilitarian background.

So, faced with their own *tabula rasa*, the Founding Fathers understood they were given a unique opportunity to create something never before done: a sustainable government focused on the people. Included in that charge was the thought that its citizens were entitled to all the basic rights that could be bestowed on an individual, including such things as intellectual property and government-granted monopolies. Such responsibility, of course, engendered heated discussions, both in person and through written correspondence. The debates surrounding the formation of our Constitution, therefore, were heavily steeped in concepts of both utilitarianism and natural laws, which particular focus on life, property, and liberty. James Madison summed up this focus perfectly when he stated:

> . . . government is instituted, and ought to be exercised for the benefit of the people; which consists in the enjoyment of life and liberty, with the right of acquiring and using property, and generally of pursuing and obtaining happiness and safety.

Madison expressed the prevailing view of the time, that the defense of liberty is integrally associated with the defense of personal property, not the least of which was intellectual property, or original thought. These concepts are so inextricably bound together that unraveling one thread will severely weaken the fabric of our society.

The Founding Fathers understood that protection of private rights in any type of property, tangible or otherwise, could not exist unless the Constitution guaranteed them. Delegates to the

Constitutional Convention frequently stressed the importance of property rights in their fervent debates, and many of their ideas ultimately ended up as provisions to the Constitution, and ultimately were expressed even more clearly in the Bill of Rights.

In the end, the delegates' exposure to the government of England led them to the conclusion the powers of their new federal government should be limited, and ultimate power would be diffused amongst the states and thus more closely aligned with the people. This would help ensure and protect the citizens' personal rights, including the right to acquire and use property, and the right to exploit the fruits produced by their exertion of labor on the property. In the next chapter, we examine the central role of property in the framework of the U.S. Republic and, in particular, our U.S Constitution.

CHAPTER 5
Property Rights

"The reason why men enter into society is the preservation of their property."

"Government has no other end, but the preservation of property."

-John Locke

As explored in the previous chapter, our Forefathers spent much of their time reading the philosophical and political writings of their day. The works they read were primarily focused on the issues of property and liberty and thus the Framers spent many hours contemplating and debating how the two concepts intersected. So, to truly understand *intellectual* property rights, *e.g., the copyright monopoly,* our understanding of the general development of real property rights and liberty must be expanded, as all of these concepts as they developed in the United States find their roots in the philosophies examined earlier. The development of a healthy construct of liberty and property rights is historically regarded as one of the institutional cores of a thriving market economy. Without these primordial ideas, developed in the writings of Smith, Locke, Bentham, and Mill, there would be no America.

Much of our Forefathers' thoughts regarding property and its entanglement with liberty developed in direct response to the so-called "financial revolution" that occurred in England, the development of central banking and creation and monetization of the public debt by the Bank of England. Almost seven centuries of British history culminated in the late 1600's into a complex system of laws and encumbrances on real property. Alongside the financial revolution, the Stationers Company of England flourished and controlled book publishing in the same way the Bank of England controlled the purse strings. Both were used at the whims of Kings and Queen to control thought.

Our Founding Fathers were witnesses to such affronts to personal freedom. Because of their heightened acuity to personal liberty, they opposed such governmental control, since liberty for them meant the absence of governmental restraint on liberty. Hence, the Framers disdained all monopolies. The response was a refocused emphasis on *real property* and the creation of ideas and institutions to support the treatment of land and of course intellectual endeavors, as actual commodities, but only in so much as society as a whole would receive a benefit.

At first blush, giving such property rights to an individual may seem counter to the philosophy of utilitarianism upon which copyright law is fundamentally based, but on closer examination, the benefits received by society in exchange for the individual rights far outweigh the sacrifices made by the whole. This is the unique realization to which our Founding Fathers arrived. So, assuming certain limitations, the concept is in line with the philosophy.

A good example of the impact of property rights on economic development can be found in the history of the Oklahoma Land Rush. The Indian Appropriations Bill of 1889, signed into law by President Benjamin Harrison, authorized him to open the two million acres for settlement. So, at high noon on April 22, 1889, an estimated 50,000 people stood ready to rush the prime real estate for their own piece of the available territory. Some "sooners" hid out in the more desirable plots and appeared at the designated time to claim the land unethically.

By the end of that day, Oklahoma City was established with a population of approximately 10,000 citizens. Newspapers reported the town was staked out and governments formed by the end of the first day. By the second week following the land rush, schools were in place and volunteers were teaching the children. Within a month, Oklahoma City had five banks and six newspapers. All of this commerce was led by the governmental establishment of property rights. Individuals literally "staked out" their claims in otherwise natural property to "fix" that to which they were entitled and they fully expected the government to support them in those rights. What was once governed by natural law, then, became subject to utilitarianism in the form of a social contract and the rights of society yielded to the rights of the individual. The Oklahoma land rush illustrates more clearly than anything that without law there can be no property rights.

Generally, the more remote the property, the greater is the degree of government enforcement necessary to maintain the individual's right. In the Oklahoma model, the structure was officially enforced either by local land offices or the U.S. Department of Interior. If a person's staked claim was in close proximity to a land office, reliance on the government enforcement would protect his interest in the property. But in the more remote portions of the territory far removed from any form of organized government, a person who staked a claim had to be prepared to enforce it individually. Where there is no mechanism for enforcement of property rights, individuals used coercive force and aggression. This concept is important in considering enforcement of intellectual property rights, as they are generally more like the latter scenario than the former in that if enforcement is to be effective, the owner of the intellectual property has to be the aggressor and cannot generally rely on the government to do the bidding.

When people discuss real property and property rights as established by a society, the question often arises as to what drives society to create laws giving persons rights to "own" property. This question is of critical importance when the leap is made from real property to intellectual property. In his work *The Law*, Frédéric Bastiat connects the concept of property ownership to very basic human needs such as life and liberty, in much the same way as did James Madison:

> Life, liberty, and property do not exist because men have made laws. On the contrary, it was the fact that life, liberty, and property existed beforehand that caused men to make laws in the first place.

Perhaps it is this association with security, itself a form of freedom, that causes people to demarcate their property with "white picket fences," the dream shared by many Americans, even though the "fact" of ownership exists beforehand. This idyllic association is a form of life that many hold up as success. We see this reflected in Bastiat's words: an almost Platonic emphasis on an ideal form of life, liberty and property which existed prior to, but was the basis of manmade laws. In other words, it is a focus on what Locke may have called a "natural law."

This natural association between security and property ownership was by no means lost on our Founding Fathers. They, too, understood the need for establishment of a system of property rights that could be enforced by the government to ensure security. Once again, their thoughts in this regard were impacted by the seminal work on the subject of property in their day, Locke's *Second Treatise on Civil Government*, which was written against the backdrop of political crisis and revolution. Both as a result of Locke's treatise and by their own experience, they were painfully aware of the tyranny often the result of a government depriving its citizens of their property. They had significant concerns about agents of the Crown barging into their private dwellings, interrogating them, and seizing their private property under the authority of a standing "warrant" from the King.

This steadfast belief in the inviolability of property, combined with their desire to eliminate any threat of future tyranny, is why our Forefathers added the Bill of Rights to the Constitution. Our 4th Amendment protects us from unlawful searches and seizures. The 5th Amendment assures no person shall "be deprived of life, liberty, or property, without due process of law; nor shall private property be taken for public use, without just compensation." It is likely the inclusion of the Bastiatian language of "life, liberty and property" is not a coincidence. The association of these three elements permeates our country's formation and its legal jurisprudence. So important are these rights they were later specifically made applicable to the states by the passage of the 14th Amendment.

The 4th Amendment stands as a glaring counter argument to the antagonists who would say intellectual property rights are not similar to real property rights. This premise can be found, for example, in the work of economists Boldrin & Levine, *Against Intellectual Monopoly*, where they write:

> [The] analogy between "idea" and "land" is false. The argument tries to portray intellectual property as nothing but standard private property adapted to the case of ideas. It is a misleading view, completely divorced from the reality of how innovations come about and of how intellectual property law functions. To begin seeing why, observe that "property of land" confers the right to use and dispose of your land as you see fit, while "intellectual property over an idea" confers the right to prohibit others from using their copies of the idea.

Boldrin & Levine then conclude that the equivocation between real property and intellectual property "equates a right to use with a right to prohibit." Quite to the contrary, the concept of a monopoly, either in an idea or in land, does not segregate those rights into distinct categories, but rather fully *includes both rights*. One who owns real property, even what Boldrin & Levine describe as "rivalrous" property such as coffee beans, has the exclusive right to exclude others from taking that property, the right to *prohibit*, as well as the right to *enjoy* it. But Boldrin & Levine claim ideas are "non-rivalrous" because one person's consumption of them does not limit others from enjoying the idea, as does one's enjoyment of coffee.

While this may at first seem a valid point, the argument fails when one considers the context of downloading a copyrighted work from the Internet: the public consumption of that work directly deprives the songwriter from the benefit of economic income from his or her expressed idea, *i.e.*, it limits the songwriters' enjoyment of his or her creation and is, therefore, rivalrous. Thus Bolden & Levine's distinctions between rights enjoyed by owners of intellectual property versus owners of real property are incorrect, particularly in the context of the idea/expression dichotomy. The function of the law in providing the rights to ownership and monopoly are, in both instances, the thing that makes the two types of property equivalent.

The importance of being able to manage, defend and control one's own property rights in an effective government is clearly evident in the writings of Jefferson. In a letter to Samuel Kerchiyal, written on July 12, 1816, he wrote:

> The true foundation of republican government is the equal right of every citizen, in his person and property, and in their management. Try by this, as a tally, every provision of our constitution, and see if it hangs directly on the will of the people.

Jefferson classifies the right of a person to manage his or her property as the foundation of republican government and suggests it as the litmus test of the Constitution. That being true, the implication is Jefferson believed management of one's property rights pursuant to the copyright clause of the Constitution would have passed the tally. Jefferson thus believed, contrary to Boldrin & Levine, the owner of a copyright should have both the right to use it and the right to prohibit others from using it.

The property rights granted to a person by the government are extensive. An owner of property has the right to control the use of the property: he or she may consume, sell, rent, mortgage, transfer, exchange or destroy the property, or to exclude others from doing these things. Owners can grant rights to persons or entities in the form of easements, licenses, and leases. The property right itself is also distinguishable, and divisible, from other rights resulting from the ownership, such as mineral, development, and air rights. If protection of these rights with regard to real property is so essential to the foundations of true republic, how much more important is the protection of these rights with regard to the less tangible intellectual properties.

If my tenet that real property and intellectual property are equal in the eyes of philosophy and law is true, then further analogies between the two will serve to inform our inquiry. Some real properties, such as national parks, land used for roadways, and governmental buildings, are sometimes referred to as "commons," *i.e.*, they are party of the "general collective ownership" of the Federal government, *i.e.*, *the people*. If the government is forced to "take" property from one of its citizens, the 5th Amendment requires the person to be compensated.

These principals underlying real property concepts are the same principals we find when talking about intellectual properties like copyright and patents. Like real property, the rights in intellectual property are divisible and their owners can lease, license, sell or otherwise dispose of them in certain ways defined by law. Like properties deemed by the government as "commons," there are also "commons" in intellectual properties: ideas, facts, and the building blocks of the creative arts, *i.e.*, words, letters, musical notes, chords, shapes, colors, paints, clay, etc., not to mention the ideas embedded in expressions disseminated by their creators, and works in the public domain. This is the continuum of thought that has existed time immemorial and will continue to exist for generations to come. The Supreme Court affirmed this principle in the unanimous decision of *Feist Publications, Inc. v. Rural Telephone Services Co.*, 499 U.S. 340 (1991) in which it ruled copyright protection only extends to creative works, not to "facts" such as those contained in a telephone book. This principle was again reaffirmed in their recent decision in *Golan v. Holder*. This continuum of thought contains the ideas that lead to thoughts and innovations which, when expressed, become copyrights.

In general, our society adheres to the principal that once a person applies a certain amount of effort to a property, the property should belong to that person. In the case of real property, we use a system of monetary exchange, earning it by the "sweat of our brows" and thereby saving enough funds to purchase the property. In the case of intellectual property, the creative efforts necessary to create the work are the efforts entitling the person to ownership of that creation.

It was actually our old friend John Locke, the advocate of natural law, who advanced this theory that when a person mixes his or her labor with nature, that person gains a relationship with that part of nature with which the labor is mixed, subject only to the limitation that there should be "enough, and as good, left in common for others." So, even though our copyright laws are actually based on the utilitarian philosophy that a great societal good is served by the creation and dissemination of original thought, this natural law principle also influences the traditional contours of the copyright construct.

The copyright monopoly is nothing more than a property right giving people the right to control and profit from their own creations so society will be motivated to create new innovations. But because of its ethereal nature, the property of copyright is sometimes a difficult concept for some people to grasp, as we saw earlier in our analysis of Bolden & Levine and as we shall see later in a detailed discussion of an article written by The Pirate Bay founder, Rick Falkvinge. In reality, the construct of owning real property is just as "evanescent" as the construct of owning intangible property. Both are mythical creations of the law or, as the Supreme Court might say, are metaphysical constructs. Ironically, neither is based in any real physical plane, but is rather creations of our minds.

When we acquire property, even real property perceived to be based on a physical plane, we only acquire the right to *control* that property for the length of time we "own" it - not unlike copyright. When we die, our ownership of the property, whether the property itself is tangible or not, dies with us. We may be entitled by law to pass it down to our heirs, but the days of our individual "ownership" in any physical plan are over. When we are food for worms, our ownership, as it were, goes up in the evanescent smoke. Simply stated, our ownership in real property, like our ownership in creative properties, is a fictitious creation of the law intended for our benefit while we are alive.

The metaphysical nature of any form of property ownership crystallizes an important component in our copyright construct: property ownership, which we have seen was closely associated with the concept of liberty, is based on the right to control. If there is no right to control, there is no ownership.

In his book, *Free Culture: The Nature and Future of Creativity*, Lawrence Lessig argues intellectual property is concentrated in the hands of a powerful few media companies who control it and keep "free culture" from accessing it. This, he says, it antithetical to our free market and free speech concepts. In reality, however, a majority of the real property ownership in America is concentrated in the "hands" of a few conglomerates and industries such as the insurance and investment cartels. Does this fact equally negate the need for our legal creation of property ownership? It is difficult to make that leap, since the essence of ownership is control and it is more antithetical to U.S. history to restrict the few from controlling the property. The concept of individual ownership benefits society as a whole. It is important here to reiterate that the concepts of free market and free speech are inextricably linked to the enforcement of monopoly ownership in property, regardless of whether it's real or intellectual.

R. G. Collingwood, in *The Principle of Art*, misses this importance of property ownership as well, particularly as it emerges in copyright law. In the conclusion to his important work on the philosophy of art, he advocates we as a society eliminate the "conception of artistic ownership" because, essentially, it is harming the artist. He wrote:

> We try to secure a livelihood for our artists (and God knows they need it) by copyright laws protecting them against plagiarism; but the reason why our artists are in such a poor way is because of that very individualism which these laws enforce.

I address Collingwoods' idea that an artist does not create in a vacuum elsewhere, but the point to be observed here is that Collingwood misses the focus of copyright law as it has developed in the U.S. The purpose of creating an "artistic ownership" is not solely to help artists defend against plagiarism, but more importantly to feed society's coffers with new art and innovation.

Another lesson we can learn from our analogy of real property to intellectual property is the former is made up of substance. It can be seen, touched, smelled, and experienced. Made up of atoms, it can be used up or transformed into another form. A person can apply labor to the land and create a garden. Land can be mined for minerals and depleted. Coal mined from land can be transformed into energy, totally consumed, or it can be converted to coke or ash. But the concept of our ownership of real property is not physical, but rather is a creation of our mind as expressed in laws.

Intellectual property differs from real property only in the sense that its existence is not necessarily on the physical plane, as is the existence of real property. Although it can be controlled and owned, through government fiat, it cannot be "possessed" in the same sense we declare a possession of real properties. Real property ownership can be defended in the physical plane in a way intellectual property cannot.

Pure intellectual property, the idea, is not identical to real property in this respect. In its natural state, you cannot smell intellectual property, nor can you see it, or touch it. And, as Jefferson intimated, as long as you keep it to yourself, an idea cannot be physically taken from you, as can real property. But once you "dispossess" yourself of the idea and share it with another, you lose the ability to inherently control the idea, and potentially the ownership of the idea: unless, of course, there is some outside authority to step in and allow you to claim ownership of the idea and physically enforce your ownership in a court of law. That is the crux of the copyright concept: products of a person's mind are just as much the creator's property as products of a person's hands. The fence we use to delineate its borders is expression. And that is the equivocation intimated earlier that it is *the control* of property that gives a person monopoly, not its existence. If we look at intellectual property in this sense, it should be valued as an asset and as protectable as real property from the moment of creation.

Many times, more labor and expenditure is invested into the expression, development, and marketing of intellectual property than in the development of real property. Successful sound recordings often cost millions of dollars to produce and market. Broadway plays can cost upwards of $5 million to produce. Hollywood movies can cost ten or more times that. There is a significant economic justification - translated in Lockean terms as application of labor - for the existence of copyright. Without the economic incentives, there would be less investment in the creative arts.

If you examine the seminal quote by Jefferson regarding ideas in specific detail, he clearly indicates his awareness of this principle. Jefferson concludes that famous diatribe about intellectual thought with these words: "Inventions then cannot, *in nature*, be the subject of property." Note the emphasis. The point Jefferson is making is that, *in their natural state*, inventions are not the subject of property, *i.e.*, ownership and control. However, with the application of law, the marvelous little original thought in our heads can be the subject of ownership and control. It was Jefferson who, in the end, agreed to the principle that providing economic incentive to society to create arts and inventions would engender innovation. It may not have been the *natural state*, but it appealed to his utilitarian philosophy.

CHAPTER 6

Engine of Free Expression

If you have an apple and I have an apple and we exchange these apples then you and I will still each have one apple. But if you have an idea and I have an idea and we exchange these ideas, then each of us will have two ideas.

-George Bernard Shaw

Granting creators an exclusive monopoly in their expression of thoughts necessarily limits the ability of others to express themselves. This, of course, butts up against the prohibition of the First Amendment that the government shall not prohibit the freedom of speech.

But rather than viewing the relationship between copyright and free speech as a conflict, the Supreme Court views the motivation behind the copyright monopoly (to provide incentive to creators) as complimentary to the purpose of the First Amendment's guarantee of free speech. In *Harper & Row v. Nation Enterprises* 471 U.S. 539 (1985), the Court summarized as follows:

> It should not be forgotten that the Framers intended copyright itself to be the engine of free expression, and only if

that engine is adequately fueled will public access to literary, musical and artistic creations be ensured. . . .

In other words, the Supreme Court believes the copyright monopoly actually *honors* and *enhances* the First Amendment. The Court reiterated this belief in recent challenges when they stated, the "traditional contours of copyright" include inherent protections for First Amendment rights. Despite this, many scholars, like Christina Bohannan in an article titled *"Copyright Harm and the First Amendment,"* attempt to argue that application of copyright law is unconstitutional as it violates the First Amendment.

In the opening sentence of the treatise, Bohannan says "Copyright law is a glaring and *unjustified* exception to the general rule that the government may not prohibit speech without a showing that the speech causes harm." This statement directly contradicts the position of the Supreme Court that the traditional scrutiny applied to government regulation of speech *do not apply* to copyright regulations which, the court said in *Eldred v. Ashcroft,* has its own "traditional contours" to protect speech. More importantly, it ignores the fact that our Forefathers, including Jefferson, believed the exception, although maybe glaring, was in fact justified by their utilitarian trade-off, *i.e.,* society trades in certain rights to free expression in order to encourage every individual to contribute to the continuum of ideas.

According to the Supreme Court in the *Eldred v. Ashcroft* decision, any free speech concerns created by the copyright laws are addressed by the limitations already in existence, defining the "traditional contours" as the idea/expression dichotomy and the fair use doctrine. They reaffirmed this in *Golan v. Holder.*

The Bohannan article accurately states that one of the reasons the Supreme Court treats free speech issues differently in the copyright context is "copyrights are property, and the First Amendment does not require property holders to let others use their property for speech purposes." Bohannan later argues against this rationale as follows:

> [T]he nature of the property right inherent in copyrights is fundamentally different from other kinds of property in ways that matter a great deal for purposes of the First Amendment. Indeed, it is because copyright law is charged with encouraging free expression that the property rights it conveys should be limited where necessary to achieve that purpose.

This distinction between the copyright monopoly and other kinds of monopolies in real property is foundational to Bohannan's argument if third-party use of a copyright does not harm the creator's incentive to create, then copyright law burdens free speech because it does not serve a compelling state interest. Unfortunately, Bohannan's arguments are flawed in almost every respect.

First, as is argued in prior chapters, the concept of a property right in an expression is fundamentally the same as the concept of property ownership in general and any attempt to unravel the two concepts threatens to shred the fibers of our Constitution and destroy our liberty. Both real property and intellectual property are government-backed monopolies granting control to the owner. Second, as is argued elsewhere, non-commercial use of copyrights has created significant harm to creators' incentive to create. Third, once again it attempts to apply a standard of scrutiny to copyright law the Supreme Court, no less, has said does not apply.

It is also argued by Bohannan and other scholars that copyright law burdens speech because it restricts what a person can say and write. But does it? Remember, copyright only protects the *expression* of an original thought, not an abstract idea itself. In 1915, a Ukranian painter by the name of Kazimir Severinovich Malevich created a work of art titled *The Black Circle*. In the philosophy of the Suprematism school of thought he founded, it was simply a painting of a black circle situated slightly to the upper right corner of a square white canvas. Does Malevich's monopoly in his creation prevent others from expressing similar ideas?

While Malevich's individual creation was certainly his own, the question that comes to mind is what can be protected in this very abstract and basic work. Certainly, the abstract idea of a circle does not belong to Malevich by virtue of his ownership of copyright. Nor do the basic colors of black and white. These are all part of the continuum of ideas available to society, free for all to use in the engine of expression.

Does Malevich's work possess a "modicum" of originality as required by our copyright laws? If you view the idea of offsetting the circle slightly to the upper right as a modicum, then the answer would be yes. I beg to differ. I would maintain that very little in Malevich's expression is original thought, entitled to copyright protection.

I use this analogy to argue against the concept that copyright law burdens speech because it restricts what a person can say and write. In the sense a person cannot *copy* my original expression, the concept is true. In the sense it restricts free speech in general, the concept is false. If I take a ferry to Staten Island and create a painting depicting New York City at night, that is free expression. It would likely possess the modicum of originality necessary to grant me a copyright monopoly. A second person, however, can stand in the exact spot on Staten Island and paint his or her expression of New York City at night without infringing my copyright. In fact, even if I and the second artist were standing side by side on the same night painting our expressions, thanks to the concept of "simultaneous creation," both of us possess a copyright monopoly in our expressions, even though both will most likely be substantially similar.

This concept may be further illustrated by two photographers standing side by side, photographing the same subject. The subject is not the subject of copyright protection but, rather, each individual photographer has a copyright in his original expression of that subject, filtered through his or her sieve of experience, through which their individual composition, exposure, and creativity pour.

These scenarios illustrate neither party's free speech rights are restricted by copyright law, since copyright law provides additional defenses allowing for these types of seemingly duplicate creations. Copyright law, then, does not prohibit anyone's original expression of an idea. What it prohibits is someone's literal *copying* of an original thought belonging to someone else. The idea that copyright law restricts free speech is therefore erroneous.

CHAPTER 7

The Utilitarian Idea of a Monopolistic Right in Intangible Property

The classical libertarian, Frédéric Bastiat, is quoted as saying:

"In the full sense of the word, man is born a proprietor. . . . Faculties are only an extension of the person; and property is nothing but an extension of the faculties. To separate a man from his faculties is to cause him to die; to separate a man from the product of his faculties is likewise to cause him to die. "

Bastiat's assertion that property is nothing more than an extension of a person's faculties is an elaboration of Locke's philosophy that man deserves to profit from the exertion of labor on property otherwise available to all. Based on similar ideas, as expanded in previous chapters, it was the intent of Madison and Jefferson, as well as the Constitutional Congress, to bestow upon creators a limited monopoly for their creations, *i.e.*, to give them a property right. Jefferson in particular, came to the conclusion that creation of the copyright monopoly served, in the end, a utilitarian goal in as much as it brings multiple benefits to society. Jefferson struggled with the intersection of natural rights and utilitarian philosophies at the corner of science and arts, but he was ultimately convinced, by Madison, there was a need for the limited monopoly in order to encourage creators to create.

So, having the ultimate governmental *tabula rasa*, our Founding Fathers wanted creativity and originality to flourish in the new country they were forming. Their hope was settlers, both men and women, would create new inventions and works of literature which would populate the new libraries being built in new cities like Philadelphia. As observed, this was not only something that would happen when the works fell out of the monopoly and into the public domain, as noted earlier, but was more importantly and foremost something they anticipated would happen immediately as the works entered into the societal stream of consciousness, or what the Germans refer to as Zeitgeist. More precisely, Zeitgeist, a term I use frequently throughout this book, is an idea first proposed by Hegel in his writing to refer to the general cultural, intellectual, ethical, spiritual, and political climate of a particular age. The benefits received by society envisioned by the Framers, therefore, occurred at the moment the new work was disseminated, not just when it fell into the public domain. In other words, unlike today's opponents of copyright emphasize, the societal benefit envisioned by the drafters is not only at the time the work fall into the public domain, but even more so when the work is created. Too much emphasize cannot be placed on this fact: our Framers believed the mere existence of the created work fueled the engine of free expression, not just its lapse from copyright protection.

The Delegates envisioned a society in which original ideas flourished in a way economist Adam Smith later described as the "marketplace of ideas." The emphasis here should be placed on the word *marketplace*, as the idea of commerce is an important component of the concept. Property is not valuable without a fluid market. When new inventions are developed, or new works of art are created, they enter the marketplace of ideas and benefit society immediately. The ideas captured and embedded in the tangible expressions instantly become components in the continuum of thought. Society does not have to wait until the works ultimately find their way into the public domain - the works may be purchased and enjoyed immediately, thereby inspiring new expressions based on those same ideas. This is not contrary to the Constitution, but is in fact the way the drafters of the Constitution envisioned it. The property right is granted to the creator for a limited time in order that the creator can benefit financially from the creation by disseminating the work so new works by other persons are created: like a möbius, the cycle has no beginning or end.

A recent article written for the blog TorrentFreak, titled *The Copyright Monopoly is a Limitation of Property Rights*, was written by none other than our friend, Rickard Falkvinge, of The Pirate Party. In this particular article, Falkvinge is either unaware of this seminal benefit given to society or he intentionally obscures it for purposes of sophistry. Falkvinge argues copyright is merely "a limitation of property rights" but is itself "not a property right." At best, that sentiment focuses on the wrong aspect of copyright law; at worse, is flat-out wrong, as I will explain in short order. It de-emphasizes the market component of the copyright monopoly as well as the liberty component of the property right. These are concepts we have seen as inextricably intertwined.

Before defending original expression against his attacks, a bit more of the background on Falkvinge and his efforts is critical for our understanding of his position. His creation, The Pirate Bay, is one of the websites responsible for perhaps more infringing musical content than any other website on the Internet. Falkvinge has criticized the Recording Industry Association of America for pointing out this fact, but several reports have shown it to be an indisputable fact. The Pirate Bay is basically a filter for BitTorrent. The site's operations were raided by the Swedish government long before the Missionary Church of Kopimism was even a twinkle in Falkvinge's eye. In response to the efforts of the creative community to protect their interests, Falkvinge founded the Swedish political party known as the "Pirate Party." The party was created ostensibly to seek "copyright reform," a misnomer which for Falkvinge really means total abolishment of creative rights, but as it has turned out, it is more focused on defending The Pirate Bay and the infringers frequenting its portal. In words taken directly from Pirate Party publications, the "political" party exists for the sole purpose of tearing down the concepts of copyright and patents and establishing a community where all ideas, whether unique or not, could be shared on file-sharing peer-to-peer networks such as The Pirate Bay. It was Falkvinge who was behind the formation of the alleged religion, Kopimism, whose primary tenets is "all information is free" and "pirating is a sacred activity." Do not think for an instance the words I am quoting are those of someone who approaches the subject from a balanced perspective. Make no mistake when you read Falkvinge, he is unabashedly biased.

As noted, Falkvinge's assertion in the TorrentFreak article that the copyright monopoly is merely a *limitation on monopoly* is incorrect. His rationale and conclusion are without any real basis in U.S. history, not to mention world philosophy. We have seen the words of Jefferson and Madison discussing the boundaries and effects of the copyright monopoly. These discussions ultimately formed the words adopted by the Convention, even absent Jefferson's attendance. In the U.S., specifically, Article 1, Section 8, Clause 8 of the United States Constitution directly refutes Falkvinge's assertion by granting Congress the power:

> To promote the Progress of Science and useful Arts, by securing for limited Times to Authors and Inventors the exclusive Right to their respective Writings and Discoveries.

The language of this grant is very clear: copyright equals a monopoly – an "exclusive right" - not a limitation. As noted earlier, our Forefathers, in this case specifically James Madison, based the idea of intellectual property rights on Mill's utilitarian philosophy. In other words, they were quite willing to constrain certain rights of society – *i.e.*, the free speech "rights" to use someone else's intellectual property however they choose – if doing so would ultimately serve to advance the greater good of society as a whole. If there is a limitation on monopoly implicit in Article 1, Section 8, Clause 8, other than the obvious limitation of time discussed later, it is the one placed on society's free speech rights. The Framers recognized that granting a monopoly in certain types of speech inherently conflicted with the rights of others to exploit that exact speech. That is the conflict between the Copyright Clause, an article of our original Constitution and the free speech clause of the first of the amendments to that document.

It should be remembered the Delegates had the unique opportunity to create a new system of government and a new society - a rare opportunity indeed - so, the original drafters of the Constitution did just that with the copyright monopoly. In this instance, they yielded to the few by giving them a monopoly, but only in exchange for receiving the societal benefits to be derived by a vibrant marketplace of ideas for the many.

It was not the goal of the Forefathers, as Falkvinge suggests, to grant only a *partial* ownership or monopoly to creators and inventors. Rather, the Constitution gives Congress the authority to "secure" to creators and inventors *"exclusive rights"* for a work derived from their intellect and creativity - there is nothing partial about these exclusive rights. The grant is in a whole monopoly.

Instead of acknowledging these philosophical bedrocks of copyright law, however, Falkvinge makes the accusatory assertion that the suggestion *copyright is a monopoly* is the "carefully chosen... rhetoric from the copyright lobby." That claim is completely false. Rather, the idea of a monopoly in unique ideas in exchange for a vibrant marketplace of ideas is a concept our Forefathers derived from the philosophies and history we examined in earlier chapters. They debated and discussed their thoughts and concerns about the concepts through the course of their correspondence, and ultimately, but carefully, chose to bestow upon authors and inventors the exclusive grant of a government monopoly. For these early leaders, the concept of a monopoly in intellectual property is based on the universally-accepted principle: a person should be entitled to reap the rewards of his or her labor exerted on any natural resource. So this concept is not the carefully chosen rhetoric of the copyright lobby, but rather is an innate belief to which most in the world would profess.

Antagonists to copyright, such as Falkvinge, often fail to grasp or rather disclaim the concept that ownership of an *intellectual property*, such as copyright and patent, is no different than ownership of *real property*, such as a person owning their own house or piece of land. In fact, both derive from the same bases, *i.e.*, both forms of ownership are based on universally-accepted beliefs as expressed through societal laws, ultimately giving the owner inherent rights to do with the property as they please. In other words, both are metaphysical, government-granted monopolies.

As we explored in more detail in the previous chapter, the government prohibits individuals from reproducing and distributing copyrighted works in exactly the same way the government prohibits individuals from trespassing onto another person's personal property or stealing their possessions. Do the latter "government-sanctioned private monopolies" related to theft of real property impose "limitations of property rights" on individuals other than the owner of the real property? Of course.

Enforcement of rights against the body politic is what a monopoly is all about: *allowing an individual entity to control something to the exclusion of all other competitors*. Again, notice the emphasis on *competition*, a free market concept. Thus, focusing on the *limitation* rights of a monopolistic property right, to the exclusion of the latter, is extremely misguided. A monopoly is useless without the ability to control it.

In an attempt to prove his thesis, Falkvinge compares a DVD containing intellectual property to the purchase of a physical object such as a chair. He says:

> When I buy a chair, I hand over money for which I get the chair and a receipt. This chair has been mass-produced from a master copy at some sort of plant. After the money has changed hands, this particular chair is mine. There are many more like it, but this one is mine. I have bought one of many identical copies and the receipt proves it.

There is a significant different between *real property* (*i.e.* the chair in Mr. Falkvinge's comparison), and a copyright (*i.e.* what is embodied on the DVD in the aforesaid comparison): the chair is a tangible object and its essence is easily grasped by our senses. You can see it, touch it, sit in it, and smell it. A DVD, on the other hand, is a physical object which embodies a movie, or intellectual property. While you can still see, touch, and smell a DVD, the intangible component - *the movie embodied on the DVD* - is more difficult to conceptualize, *i.e.*, it cannot, without some mechanism to aid it, be seen, touched or smelled. This is where the wheels fall off Falkvinge's comparative analysis.

When purchasing a copyrighted work such as a movie, one has to realize the two forms of property contained or embodied within that physical object that is the DVD. Falkvinge seems to miss this fact as he draws his analogy between the chair and the DVD. He says, "[w]hen I buy a movie, I hand over money and I get the DVD and a receipt . . . after the money has changed hands, *this particular movie is mine.*" (Emphasis added). If this were a logical syllogism, as most arguments are, Falkvinge has committed the fallacy of equivocation, *i.e.*, a movie = DVD. His statement that he owns *the particular movie* is factually and legally incorrect. The correct syllogism is movie ≠ DVD. Mr. Falkvinge does not own the particular movie; rather he merely owns the physical embodiment of the movie, the DVD, not the movie itself. To use an earlier analogy, he owns the wine skins, but not the wine.

Although the purchaser owns the *physical embodiment* of the DVD – and in fact may dispose of it any way he or she chooses in accordance with the first sale doctrine – the purchaser *does not own* the *intellectual property* embodied within the DVD, and *may not* exercise dominion, or monopoly, over that property. According to U.S. copyright law, only the creator of the work owns the *intangible property* encoded in the DVD. Only that creator may, according to section 106 of the United Sates Copyright Code, make copies in order to reproduce and distribute the work. Only the creator of the intellectual property holds the monopoly therein. The owner of the physical object containing the movie has no such rights. Our Constitution - our founding doctrine - is what controls this fact, not just the copyright laws Congress has passed under the authority of the Constitution.

The umbrella of intellectual property - more specifically Article I, Section 8, Clause 8 of the Constitution - also includes under its monopoly the concept of patents. In the article, when Falkvinge compares the limitations copyright places on the purchaser of a DVD to the endless opportunities an ostensibly-expired patent gives the purchaser, he erroneously concludes "patents are not relevant for this discussion." Oh, but they are. One cannot legitimately compare a patent whose monopoly has expired to a copyrighted work currently retaining its monopoly, *i.e.*, its exclusive rights. As we have seen from the Constitutional foundations of intellectual property rights, no discussion of government-granted monopolies would be complete without incorporating the concept of patents.

One author has asserted that it is, in fact, patents and not copyrights that place a greater restriction, or monopoly, on property rights. In *Man, Economy, and State*, Murray Rothbard concluded:

> The patent is incompatible with the free market precisely to the extent that it goes beyond the copyright.... The crucial distinction between patents and copyrights, then, is not that one is mechanical and the other literary. The fact that they have been applied that way is an historical accident and does not reveal the critical difference between them. The crucial difference is that copyright is a logical attribute of property right on the free market, while patent is a monopoly invasion of that right.

Although I do not necessary subscribe to Rothbard's conclusive distinction between copyright and patent, his point is well taken that businesses should not be restricted from independently designing and creating a product using natural laws and principles, even if it turns out to be similar to a patented product, even though our legal structure often operates in that manner. What Rothbard refers to as "natural laws and principles" I have been describing as the continuum of thought and I agree those should belong to no person.

In many letters and opinions drafted by Thomas Jefferson, it is apparent he, too, was concerned with giving monopolies to products using natural laws and principles, simply because their discovery was preeminent in priority. In an 1813 letter to Isaac McPherson, Jefferson discussed this issue in the context of the use of a system of buckets by Egyptians and the Persians to raise and move water and its similarity to a patent owned by Mr. Oliver Evans. Jefferson wrote:

> [If a] string of buckets is invented and used for raising water, ore, etc., can a second have a patent rights to the same machine for raising wheat, a third oats, a fourth rye, a fifth peas, etc.? The question whether such a string of buckets was invented first by Oliver Evans is a mere question of fact in mathematical history.

His experiences as the first examiner of the Patent Office and as an inventor himself taught Jefferson that an invention should be *novel* in order to be protected by the Constitutional monopoly. Jefferson's concerns notwithstanding, the greater point to be made here is this: accepting the validity of a patent monopoly requires the acceptance of a copyright monopoly. Both rights are granted by the same Constitutional clause and, *a priori*, both are relevant to any discussion of government-granted monopolies. Copyright may be based on originality, while patent is based on novelty, but simply stated, it's all for one and one for all: the monopolies of copyright and patent stand or fall together, Constitutionally speaking.

Falkvinge's quick dismissal of the concept of patents thus is simply a persuasive device intended to diminish any discussion of the chair's patent-ability, which is the cornerstone of his argument. Simply because an individual purchases the physical embodiment of a chair design does not imply acquisition of the full rights to disassemble, analyze, reengineer, and distribute the chair commercially. Again, the chair is no longer under the protection of the patent monopoly, but is rather part of the marketplace of ideas, just as our Forefathers intended.

So, let's play with Falkvinge's analogy, imagining that, instead of the chair, we are purchasing a new automobile, a Ford Mustang. Does the person who purchases an automobile by virtue of that sales transaction, gain the right to reconstruct and reverse engineer the product, and start his or her own manufacturing facility to churn out duplicate cars in order to compete with Ford? He too, like Falkvinge, possesses a receipt for his purchase. Does he not possess the right to make copies of the car? Obviously the answer is no, but why is this situation different from Falkvinge's DVD? It's simple: there is intellectual property embodied in the automobile just as intellectual property is embodied in a DVD, a CD and, yes, even an MP3 or an MP4. Purchase of the physical, tangible embodiment of an expressed idea does not grant the purchaser a monopoly in that expression.

In a few years, when 3-D scanning and printing technologies, otherwise known as CAD-CAM, decrease in price, the same controversies being aired about copyright will arise regarding patents and retail products. This technology will soon allow a consumer to go online, select and purchase a retail item such as a wristwatch, download the specification to the computer, and "print" the object minutes later through a sophisticated process of extrusion. Falkvinge's The Pirate Bay has already established a category on their site for so-called "physibles" allowing users to exchange illegally-obtained specifications for 3-D objects. As explained earlier, Falkvinge is already at the forefront of assuring digital thieves will be equally able to do this by providing a section of The Pirate Bay where these specifications can be traded illegally. But even this technology, while certainly an affront to the principles of utilitarianism for which we argue, will not eliminate the historical underpinnings of copyright and patent; nor will it change society's belief that a person should be able to exploit their creation, in this case the specifications for the wristwatch. Social contract enforces the idea those specifications are the intellectual property of the creators.

Whether there is a specific realization that these intellectual concepts are based on the utilitarian teachings of John Stuart Mill, multiple research studies illustrate society's belief that *rewarding an individual for the "fruits of their labor"* is a principle that should be enforced by social contract. When labor is applied to raw goods by an individual in order to create an original expression of an idea, our society has agreed - in the form of societal laws - that this product is the property of the individual who created it. Our Constitution grants the creator of such product a limited monopoly in the exploitation of that creation.

So, intellectual property, be it copyright, patent or trademark, is a "government-sanctioned private monopoly." It is based on an exchange of promises and consideration. It is a binding social contract, nothing more or nothing less. The ideology behind the monopolization of intellectual property is to promote and incentivize people to create works with the understanding and confidence the time, energy, and financial hardship involved will be fairly compensated. In turn, society will gain access to inventions and creations which, in turn, spawns more invention and creation. Without any supreme authority overseeing and protecting the interests and livelihood of creators, the motivation to develop such works arguably decreases dramatically. If it does, society suffers. So yes, the implementation of the monopoly bestows certain property rights to the creator, but it also provides an explicit benefit to society. And yes, as with all property rights, that grant places limitations on the persons who do not own the property. In other words, society has done a cost-benefit analysis and deemed that such a trade-off is essential and beneficial.

So, the premise maintained by copyright antagonists such as Falkvinge that the concept of copyright monopoly is an evil one which the lobbyist have attempted to associate with a positive word such as property is a weak argument, historically, philosophically, and logically. Frankly, it is flat out wrong. Rather, the positive concept of monopoly has been with us since the Code of Hammurabi first described laws regarding property; it was passed down to the U.S. by our Merry Old Ancestors from England; and it is a right the participants of the Oklahoma Land Rush had to fight to exercise. Jefferson maintained:

> [T]he tranquility, the happiness and security of mankind, rest on justice or the obligation to respect the rights of others. The respect of others for our right of domain and property is the security of our actual possessions.

This monopolistic and perhaps natural right — the right to exercise control over one's property, including one's intellectual creations — serves a utilitarian goal which assures a cohesive society in which ownership of property is exercised by the appropriate party, benefitting the greater good by supporting its liberty. This is done, simply, by wielding their monopoly against those who would steal it away. In this case, utilitarianism is served by providing the individual with control over their property, benefitting the whole by creating a nation of certainty and prosperity - a nation of liberty. The United States, unlike any other nation, has proven the truth of our Founding Father's grand experiment by producing the most vibrant "engine of free expression" in history, flowing with the milk and honey that comes from incentivizing creativity. Our nation's legacy includes many great, inventive visionaries, such as Steve Jobs, who have built a culture of creativity and a treasure chest of intellectual property that has, indeed, changed the world. The U.S. produces the bulk of music vehemently sought after in most other countries. The facts produced by the grand experiment seem to have established the theory propounded by the Framers.

Not surprisingly, Falkvinge's thoughts and assertions in this instance are decidedly not original: other antagonists argue the copyright monopoly should be invalidated as contrary to free market principles. They maintain, unlike physical property like Falkvinge's chair, intellectual property is not scarce, but rather is a legal fantasy created by the government, like the stories of Santa Clause many tell our children and, as such, cannot be exhausted.

Boldrin and Levine describe the equivocation of piracy and theft as the "silliest and easiest" argument to dismiss, concluding "it does not require a Ph.D. in economics to see that downloading music, copyrighted or not, is quite different from theft in the ordinary sense of the word." Infringing on a copyright, they argue, unlike theft, does not deprive the victim of the original item. As such, enforcement of copyright law constitutes aggression on the part of the state, and is therefore actually anti-utilitarian in that it is antagonistic to free market. This is just a different form of Falkvinge's argument that copyright is not a monopoly, but rather a limitation on property. These conclusions ignore the natural law premises undergirding much of the original thinking about copyright monopolies.

In the instance of copyright law, natural law and utilitarian law dance an intricate waltz. The arguments that copyright law is a limitation on property or antagonistic to utilitarianism obscures the philosophical underpinnings we have been so careful to build. Any limitations on society imposed by the copyright monopoly contribute significantly toward society's prosperity and commerce. This contribution actually advances the utilitarian goal of preserving liberty. Boldrin, Levine and Falkvinge do not discuss this connection in their attacks on copyright law.

Boldrin and Levine also err in their assumption that enforcement of copyright is state aggression. It is not. Enforcement of copyright is generally the responsibility of the creator, not the government, and thus any aggression is not unlike the owner of a home defending it with force against any would be intruders. We as a society not only believe that is acceptable, we often applaud those who defend their property as exercising their Constitutional rights. Why should it be considered patriotic to defend our real property homestead, but viewed as "state aggression" when we defend our intellectual property homesteads? The clear conclusion is both are equally patriotic. It is the nature of a monopoly, whether it be in real or intellectual property, that it must be defended.

So yes, a copyright monopoly creates limitations that can be used aggressively, but these limitations and aggressions are levied first and foremost against third parties who would seek to dispossess the owner of a monopoly, whether it be intellectual property or real property. The greatest limitation is, in fact, on those who would steal the intellectual rights away from their creators or inventor, just as a homeowner limits the burglar who would deprive him of life, liberty, and happiness. The inherent right of enforcement compliments, rather than lessens, the impact of a monopoly that is very real. Enforcement is the only means by which the owner can exercise his or her intellectual property rights, just as criminal laws serve to preserve his or her personal property.

So if this is a limitation on society's rights to freely distributed copyrighted product belonging to another, the majority of society seems very comfortable with that limitation: a limitation on a usurper's right to take property not belonging to him or her in order to preserve the very basis of all liberties we so enjoy - the right to life, happiness, and the pursuit of happiness.

As the French economist François Quesnay succinctly said: "Without that sense of security which property gives, the land would still be uncultivated." In other words, if we don't grant a monopoly to our cultivators of ideas, the landscape will be baron.

CHAPTER 8

The Spirit Moves in Mysterious Ways

Where the spirit does not work with the hand there is no art.

— Leonardo Da Vinci

Above all, we are coming to understand that the arts incarnate the creativity of a free people. When the creative impulse cannot flourish, when it cannot freely select its methods and objects, when it is deprived of spontaneity, then society severs the root of art.

— John Fitzgerald Kennedy

The concept that an expressed idea belongs to the person who expressed it is not a recent construct. We saw that Locke and others developed philosophies based on the idea, but these were later iterations of a universally and historically-accepted concept. One of its earliest iterations is said to have caused the famous "Battle of the Books" in the early 6th Century Ireland.

Columba was a famous Scottish saint who studied for the priesthood under St. Finnian. He loved books and was in the habit of making copies of any he could get his hands on: Psalters, Bibles, and other valuable manuscripts for his monks. One day, St. Finnian brought the first copy of St. Jerome's Psalter back from a trip to Rome. Though he treasured and guarded this volume, Finnian gave Columba permission to examine it. Columba took these opportunities to surreptitiously copy the work for his own use. Once he found out, Finnian claimed the copy belonged to him and insisted that Columba give it up. Columba refused and thus the question of ownership was brought before King Diarmaid, the Overlord of Ireland. Who owned the intellectual property? His decision in this early "copyright" case went against Columba. In his "ruling," King Diarmaid stated:

> To every cow her calf and to every book its son-book. Therefore the copy you made, O Colum Cille, belongs to Finnian.

Thus, King Diarmaid's legal reasoning appears to be an early precursor to our utilitarian model of copyright monopoly based on the Hobbesian idea of "giving to every man his own."

But many antagonists of copyright law will make the argument that these incentives elaborated earlier, as envisioned by our Forefathers in their monopoly construct, are not necessary to motivate artists and inventors to create. They argue that creation of art and literature historically occurs even in the absence of financial motivators. Dr. Lawrence Lessig, for example, often claims it is only the 20th Century that views intellectual property as a monopoly entitling its creators to "lock up" their creations in exchange for compensation. In my opinion, Dr. Lessig confuses the propensity of the United States population in the 20th Century for bringing litigation to solve problems with the efficiency of intellectual property as a monopoly, but I'm getting ahead of our discussion. Our friends Michele Boldrin and David K. Levine also jump on this bandwagon. In another article titled *Why Napster is Right*, they make the following claim:

> Historical evidence, for starters, suggests that at least when it comes to music, literature and painting/sculpture, lack of copyright protection may not matter very much. Neither at the time of Dante nor at that of Shakespeare or Michelangelo copyright laws were available [*sic*]. The same applies to Homer, the Gregorian Chants, Monteverdi and almost everything worth either reading or listening to. Still, and in spite of the much less favorable economic conditions, an enormous amount of great art of all kinds was created, which we still admire, read, listen to and ... reproduce without bothering much about copyrights.

Not only is this view historically and factually inaccurate, but it fails to recognize the economies of creation, which is surprising considering it is written by two economists. Contrary to the assertions above, much of the art, music, and literature, *i.e.,* "almost everything worth either reading or listening to," was created because the authors and creators were rewarded, either directly or indirectly, by either the admiring public or by individual benefactors, both of which recognized the value of the intangible assets with which they were confronted. In other words, the creators were incentivized to create by financial gain. Regardless of whether you call it copyright, this is the founding philosophy inspiring our Forefathers to include Article 1, Section 8, Clause 8 in the Constitution.

Many early creators, including such giants as Mozart, Leonardo da Vinci, and Michelangelo, sought and enjoyed the support of noble or ecclesiastical patrons. Mozart, for example, was supported by the Roman Catholic Church, specifically the Archbishop of Salzbur and, later the Archbishop Colloredo of Vienna. The King of France supported Da Vinci, particularly in his old age. The very prominent and influential Medici family of Florence supported Michelangelo from the time he was a young artist.

As early as the 1600's, many creators, including the most notable, William Shakespeare, exploited their works under formative laws similar to our existing copyright construct. While a law with the word "copyright" in it would not exist for another one hundred years or so, the idea of owning a monopoly in your creation was certainly part of the legal evolution and public thought.

Historical records indicate Shakespeare's plays were performed in London as early as 1592, assumedly as was the custom in those days in exchange for payment and possibly a share of the door. It is also clear in historical records that Shakespeare was an owner in a theatrical company, called "Lord Chamberlain's Men," which became the leading playhouse in London during that time. In other words, Shakespeare derived income from his labor of creation.

In 1603, Shakespeare's company was awarded a royal patent by King James I, at which time the owners changed the name to the "King's Men." Furthermore, a collection of twenty of his works, the *First Folio*, was published under this letter patent by the Stationers Company in 1623. So, to say Shakespeare created at a time before copyright law was available, though technically true as far as the actual law is concerned, is quite misleading, as he did in fact function under a similar construct: the predecessor, in fact, to the Statute of Anne. He no doubt was allowed to profit from the fruits of his intellectual labor.

These two models - the patronage model and the monopoly model - co-existed for hundreds of years prior to the actual passage of copyright laws in the early 1700's. These models provided adequate incentive for the production of the works of art with which we are familiar. This is why I indicated earlier Lessig's statement that the incentive system is unique to the 20th Century is historically inaccurate.

It is difficult to know what else may have been created in Shakespeare's period of time by the masses of people who *did not* have financial incentive, because it is this very funding that propelled society's awareness of the wise peoples' creations. But for the Medici's, the works of Michelangelo might have fallen into the vast sea of anonymity. But for the fact his collected works were published under the authority of the King's stationer, we would not have any extant copies of Shakespeare's works. So, to conclude the possession of a monopoly does not motivate creators to create is historically inaccurate. More importantly, to say providing this monopoly, a prerequisite to the investment of money, does not benefit society, is even more inaccurate from the standpoint of history. Society would simply not possess Shakespeare's works but for the monopoly given to the Stationers Company. Period.

As da Vinci said, "Where the spirit does not work with the hand there is no art." I exercise some creative liberty by interpreting the spirit in this quote to mean the creative soul, and the hand to mean, at least to some extent, the financial

127

incentive. I realize of course that this is likely not what da Vinci intended to convey, but it does at least illustrate the point made: without a financial means of fueling the flame of art and invention, the flame will die.

CHAPTER 9

Double Vision

"The natural progress of things is for liberty to yield and government to gain ground."

-Thomas Jefferson

If there is one point that needs to be stressed more than any other in defense of protecting original thought, it is that our intellectual property system is founded on both the creation of new ideas and the protection of our market place of ideas. Both are equally important and we cannot have one without the other. The fact that this balance is critical to our copyright construct is reiterated throughout the book.

But one of the primary arguments levied against the concept of copyright in the U.S. is that the length of the monopoly, intended by the drafters of the Constitution to be "for a limited time" has been amended eleven times, increasing the duration from an initial period of 14 years, to 28, to 56, to the length it is now: for the life of the author plus seventy years. In short, as intimated in the Jefferson quote above, it is argued that society's liberties, the rights to useful arts and inventions, are being curtailed by the government.

The last term extension, the Sonny Bono Copyright Extension Act, is the most controversial. Here lies the crux of the problem in the current debate as perceived by copyright's opponents. Falkvinge, Lessig, and Gaylor each make their propositions in the context of trying to solve that perceived problem with *current* copyright laws. The complaint can be summarized as follows: because the length of protection has been extended several times over the years, there are fewer and fewer works going into to public domain and, therefore, fewer ideas from which to borrow to create still new ideas. So, in the current state of the affairs, only works created *prior* to 1923 are irrevocably and indisputably in the public domain. As one scholar stated it in the converse, "no one in the last century has seen an original work created in her lifetime fall into the public domain." This is then deemed a violation of First Amendment rights of free speech because it deprives us of the right to freely use the material that remains protected by the monopoly.

In his book, *Free Culture*, Dr. Lessig stated the problem of extending the term as follows: ". . . if Congress has the power to extend existing terms [of the copyright monopoly], then the Constitution's requirement that terms be 'limited' will have no practical effect . . . . The end result of that, according to Lessig, is "Congress can achieve what the Constitution plainly forbids . . . ." But the Supreme Court disagreed with Lessig. He argued the case of *Eldred v. Ashcroft*, the case which challenged the Copyright Term Extension Act, before the Supreme Court and lost.

These pervasive arguments are not entirely without merit and mirror some of the same concerns as our Forefathers, personified by Jefferson, which arose out of very recent experiences witnessed directly by our early founders. Many of the men who drafted the Constitution were vividly aware of the history of the British government in their dealings with monopolies over intellectual properties. British history is replete with examples of the Crown, mostly Queen Elizabeth and King James, granting monopolies in the form of Letters Patent to favored subjects. In fact, the British monarchy still owns a "Crown Copyright" in the King James Version of the Bible. For the most part, however, the 1624 Statute of Monopolies was passed as means of curbing such royal abuses. It restricted patents for new inventions to a specified term of years.

In the world of English literature, the Stationers' Company, an assembly of London booksellers which received charter from the Crown held an exclusive monopoly on publishing. They maintained a register and when one of the booksellers listed a work on the register, that company held the exclusive right to copy that work, hence the origin of the word copyright. The Stationers' Company continued to enforce their monopoly, primarily through censorship, until 1695. During this period, the individual titles identified on the register were treated as perpetual properties. The Statute of Anne, passed in 1709, effectively broke up these monopolies by imposing strict term limits on copyright, even those held by the Stationers' Company. Over the following two decades, booksellers' attempts to persuade Parliament to preserve their monopolies by extending the copyright term, but these attempts were rebuffed. This backdrop informed the anti-monopoly movement in the United States and the Statute of Anne's time limitations on the copyright monopoly were adopted in the first U.S. Copyright Act of 1790.

As a result of the myriad extensions to the original term of copyright occurring throughout the history of America, current "artists" like Gregg Gillis, p/k/a "Girltalk" who use pre-existing copyright sound recordings to "mash" together and "create" new songs lament the fact they have very few so-called popular songs with which to work. So, the argument goes, artist like Girltalk should not be punished for doing what the Forefathers intended all along, using existing thought to create new thought. After all, the concept of the "public domain," also known as the "marketplace of ideas," has been around since the beginning of copyright. In a case dating back to 1615, *The Clothworkers of Ipswich*, the Court held:

> [I]f a man hath brought in a new invention and a new trade within the kingdom, . . . or if a man hath made a new discovery of any thing, . . . [the Crown] may grant by charter unto him, that he only shall use such a trade . . . for a certain time. . . .

> [B]ut when that patent is expired, the King cannot make a new grant thereof; for when the trade is become common, and others have been bound apprentices in the same trade, there is no reason that such should be forbidden to use it.

> 78 Eng. Rep. 147 (K.B. 1615).

The argument of opponents, then, is the public domain is a right of which, by virtue of the many extensions to the term of copyright by the government, the citizens are being deprived. This is the argument we saw earlier made by the petitioner in the recent case of *Golan v. Holder*, that society owns the public domain. This foundation of the argument ignores the fact, stressed earlier, that the Constitution and Copyright laws implemented under its authority are based, in principle at least, on *both* the creation *and* dissemination of new ideas and the protection of the marketplace of ideas. Again, one is no good without the other. To reiterate, the focus of our Framer as on the entry of works into the marketplace of ideas, by means of the incentive, not on the entry of the works into the public domain *after* the copyright expired. Once a new work is disseminated, society benefits by being able to utilize the ideas embedded clothed by the expression.

In *Remix*, Lessig argues in favor of placing additional limitations on the copyright monopoly. He cautions that exercising control of the monopoly in our current cultural environment - a culture in which young people are using copyrighted works at their whim to create mash ups - only results in the *criminalization* of copying ideas and imprisonment or punishment of our youth. This, he says in a slippery slope argument, will only serve to "drive them further underground." We can't stop it, says Lessig. As a result, Lessig maintains we should simply deregulate amateur creativity and decriminalize file sharing on the Internet. In his words we should "chill the 'control freaks.'" Proposals such as these are why - no surprise - Lessig is considered by the Internet culture to be one of the "hippest" lawyers on the planet, according to Gaylor. As we have seen, however, without control there can be no property and without property, there can be no liberty.

In order to provide a means by which these mash-up artists can flourish, Lessig jumps in to save the day through his creation of the "creative commons" licensing structure. It is no secret

Creative Commons is built on the principles of the existing Copyright Act in that it is a form of license for use of some or all of the rights of a copyright owner: thus an author can, for example, issue a non-exclusive license allowing anyone to freely use his or her work, with the only requirement being proper attribution. These *non-exclusive* licenses create what Creative Commons described as a "digital commons, a pool of content that can be copied, distributed, edited, remixed, and built upon, all within the boundaries of copyright law."

Hopefully you recognize by now that Lessig's "digital commons" is the same environment the Framers envisioned would be created by dissemination of original thought in the form of protected, monopolized expression. The Creative Commons isn't a new idea, but rather a recasting of our Forefathers' premises and it does nothing more than what copyright law does: ideas, concepts, and all other components of the continuum of thought are already available for the public to use freely.

Unfortunately, by attempting to circumnavigate the monopoly that is copyright and get works into this digital public domain (*i.e.*, the original creative commons) earlier than anticipated by our Forefathers, Lessig's Creative Commons methodology *effectively guts the copyright monopoly*. Issuing a *non-exclusive* license eliminates the possibility of issuing an *exclusive* license, which is the most profitable mean by which a copyright owner can profit from the creation of his or her work. In effect, the incentive devised by our Forefathers in the copyright construct is eliminated. It is perhaps for this reason, ironically enough, Lessig copyrights *all* his own books and has, to date at least, not issued a Creative Commons license for his book

Remix! It would seem Lessig is now the control freak in as much as he is taking advantage of the very copyright monopoly he criticizes. The reason, of course, is because Lessig does not want his expression of the ideas to be copied anymore than any other creator does. It is interesting how the validity of one's argument is swayed when it becomes personal.

Concerning the opponent's argument works are no longer falling into the public domain, while it may be true that extending the period of protection has the effect of slowing the process of populating the public domain with creative works, the fact is our Forefathers clearly anticipated and struggled with the possibility the limited time might be extended. Because of his belief that "ideas should spread freely" and "ideas are not, *by nature*, the subject of property," Jefferson and Madison had several exchanges in which they discussed how limited the monopoly must be. Notwithstanding his concerns that the time limitation be specified - he suggested a term of 19 years - Jefferson and his colleagues ultimately built what they considered the appropriate safeguards into the copyright provision of the Constitution (Article I, Section 8, Clause 8), providing that Congress may protect the works of "authors and inventors" for "*a limited time.*" What this tells us from an interpretive standpoint is the Forefathers *intentionally* left the phrase vague to allow future generations the opportunity to define it for themselves in the context of their time and needs. The Supreme Court has made this argument several times in responses to the many challenges to the extension over the years.

In *Eldred v. Ashcroft*, the case argued by Lessig, the Supreme Court recognized that the Forefathers did not define the phrase "for a limited time" and interpreted this as an intentional omission, giving Congress the right to define it so long as they did not create an unlimited term. So, while one can perhaps argue the period of limited time has been grossly exaggerated by extending it to the current duration of life plus seventy years for the copyright monopoly, one cannot argue that the public domain concept so carefully crafted by our Forefathers has, simply by virtue of these extensions, been abolished or, in Lessig's case, needs to be replaced. To the contrary, Madison, Jefferson, and crew knew precisely what they were doing.

The Supreme Court also noted that the Constitution is a single document containing both the Copyright Clause and the First Amendment and these two clauses, although dealing with distinct issues, seek related objectives: the creation and dissemination of information. That is the perceived paradox between the clauses. The First Amendment is triggered whenever the copyright monopoly is extended to provide new exclusive rights, new forms of expression, or new term limits not previously granted, and as such a heightened scrutiny will apply any time Congress exercises its copyright power. In support of our Founding Fathers' construct that liberty and property rights are closely intertwined, the Court has long maintained the two must work in tandem, mutually reinforcing each other, serving as an "engine of free expression." *Harper & Row, Publishers, Inc. v. Nation Enterprises*, 471 U. S. 539, 558 (1985). It is in this manner that the Supreme Court correctly resolved the paradox.

Many antagonists use the scarcity of the public domain created by the term extensions as a platform for criticism, as can be seen in a post on Duke University's Center for the Study of the Public Domain titled *What Could Have Entered the Public Domain on January 1, 2012?* The article identifies many works that would have fallen into the public domain under the 1909 U.S. Copyright Act had the extensions not been passed. One example given, *The Magician's Nephew*, written by C.S. Lewis as part of the popular *Chronicles of Narnia* series, actually serves to illustrate how extending time limitations benefits society by encouraging authors to continue to create. The next to last work in that series was written late in Lewis' life, 1956, just 8 years before he died at the age of 64. Lewis continued to produce many works right up until his death, including some of his popular works, *A Grief Observed, Letters to Malcolm: Chiefly on Prayer*, and *Screwtape Proposes a Toast*. The addition of a limited time after death, now seventy years, is designed to encourage authors, like Lewis, to continue to produce works that will generate income for their descendants even after their deaths. No one can argue Lewis' *Chronicles of Narnia* have not been hugely popular. The films and other products generated since his death have produced massive income for his estate, now controlled by the C.S. Lewis Company Ltd. This work also illustrates the important concept, pointed out by the Supreme Court, that even the monopoly element of copyright is intended as the engine of free expression, as is evidenced by the copious number of current children's works arguably inspired by the copyrighted classics, including children's literature series such as Daniel Handler's *A Series of Unfortunate Events*, and J. K. Rowling's *Harry Potter*.

Focusing only on the duration of the copyright monopoly, therefore, ignores these benefits of encouraging the creation of art in an author's advanced years and feeding the marketplace of ideas. It also ignores limitations inherent in the current copyright laws that help balance its use as an agent of censorship, *i.e.*, restricting the idea from entering the continuum of knowledge. Not only is it limited by the Constitution in its duration, it is also limited by the current implementation of the Copyright Clause, the 1976 Copyright Act as amended, to a handful of exclusive rights: distribution, reproduction, adaptation, display, and performance. One of those rights, the right of distribution, is also limited by the "first sale doctrine," which applies to the physical embodiment of the idea, *i.e.*, when I sell you this book containing my ideas, I cannot restrict you from reselling the copies you first purchased from me.

In addition, the concept of a copyright monopoly is limited by the quasi-right of fair use which actually defined in the current Copyright Act as a defense to an infringement action. The concept of fair use doctrine is actually grounded in an equitable notion, *i.e.*, that certain types of copying are permissible provided that they are "fair and bona fide." The concept was first applied by Justice Story in the 1841 decision of *Folsom v. Marsh,* 9 F.Cas. 342 (1841). Thus, the fair use doctrine allows inherently reasonable usages of the copyright monopoly for certain purposes akin to free speech, such as criticism, commentary, education, parody, etc.

Certain limitations are implicit in the definition of copyright in the current 1976 Copyright Act, that a person only possesses a copyright in the *tangible expressions* of ideas, not in mere ideas or facts isolated from those expressions. While some scholars maintain this idea arose in the 19th Century Supreme Court case of *Baker v. Selden*, 101 U.S. 99 (1879), the idea/expression dichotomy is actually inherent in the writings of Madison and Jefferson, and has been part of the copyright law construct from the beginning.

Another principle from copyright jurisprudence illustrates the concept that mere facts or ideas are not entitled to copyright protection is *scènes à faire* which, translated roughly from the French means "scenes to be made." The doctrine has been defined as "incidents, characters or settings which are as a practical matter indispensable, or at least standard, in the treatment of a given topic." For example, if a person is writing a novel set in Philadelphia, there will likely be elements demanded by that setting, such as references to South Philly, the Italian Street Market, South Street, Kelly Drive, Philly cheesesteak, etc. etc. Those elements, since they are demanded "by the scene," are considered part of the "marketplace of ideas" and may be used by other writers, even after the initial writer has expressed them in a tangible format. Similar allowances apply to things like themes of a book, certain melodic expression in a musical composition, and elements in a painting of a common subject. Such mere ideas and facts are said to be "the common property of the world." Over the years, the U.S. court system has developed such doctrines in an admirable effort to adhere to the Jeffersonian concept that an idea should not be restricted by monopoly.

This restriction that an idea is not entitled to protection under copyright law, but the tangible expression of an idea is entitled to protection is known as the idea/expression dichotomy, and it is specifically codified in Section 102(b) of the Copyright Act, which states any "idea, procedure, process, system, method of operation, concept, principle, or discovery, regardless of the form in which it is described, explained, illustrated, or embodied in such work."

The judicial and legislative doctrines of the idea/expression dichotomy, first sale, fair use, tangible expression, and *scènes à faire* stand out as very clear limitations on the copyright monopoly, specifically designed to maintain the delicate balance our Forefathers tried to achieve. They share the explicit recognition the monopolistic rights of the creator ought to be balanced against the need of society to access the creator's copyrighted work freely. They create a scale which, when tipped in favor of the society's interest, provide access to otherwise inaccessible copyright monopolies. Under these circumstances, the creator's material is considered *already part of the continuum of thought*, and therefore accessible by society as an exercise of their free speech rights. In this way, these limitations are powerful components of the current copyright construct often overlooked when the intense focus remains on the limited time language of the copyright clause or solely on the works that have fallen into the public domain. As with any textual exegesis, overemphasis on one word or phrase in a text will often lead to misinterpretation.

In short, all of these limitations, not *just the limitation of time*, were implemented, in the spirit of Jefferson, so the beneficiaries of the copyright monopoly, *i.e.*, the public, "will not be permanently deprived of the fruits of an artist's labors." *Stewart v. Abend*, 495 U. S. 207, 228 (1990). The Supreme Court has said the copyright monopoly exists as a reward, not to provide a private benefit to an individual, but rather for the utilitarian purpose of stimulating creativity for the good of society. See also, *Sony Corp. of America v. Universal City Studios, Inc.*, 464 U. S. 417, 429 (1984); *Twentieth Century Music Corp. v. Aiken*, 422 U. S. 151, 156 (1975). Thus, the *reward* of a copyright monopoly is intended to be consequential, a means to an end: to inspire the creation and dissemination of original ideas.

As Madison noted, giving a monopoly to authors and inventors for their creations was justified for two reasons: (1) because it was "compensation for," *i.e., a reward,* for an actual community benefit; and (2) because the monopoly was temporary, limited by the Constitution in time. *Madison on Monopolies* 756. Madison concluded "under that limitation a sufficient [compensation] and encouragement may be given." In *The Federalist* No. 43, Madison wrote:

> The utility of this power will scarcely be questioned. The copy right of authors has been solemnly adjudged in Great Britain to be a right of common law. The right to useful inventions seems with equal reason to belong to the inventors. The public good fully coincides in both cases with the claims of individuals.

Finally, in a manuscript published posthumously in 1914, Madison summarized:

> The Constitution of the U.S. has limited them to two cases, the authors of Books, and of useful inventions, in both which they are considered *as a compensation for a benefit actually gained to the community as a purchase of property which the owner otherwise might withhold from public use.* There can be no just objection to a temporary monopoly in these cases; . . . because under that limitation a sufficient recompense and encouragement may be given. . . (Emphasis added).

Thus, according to the general writings of the man who had the most instrumental influence on the words of the Constitution, the primary objective of the copyright monopoly was to reward the author or inventor, not so much for giving him or her financial gain, but rather as an incentive to secure public benefits derived from the authors' labors *both at the time the work is created,* and *again when the work passes into the public domain.* Society is therefore the recipient of two rewards in exchange for the monopoly.

Understanding this *dual benefit to society* is critical in analyzing and justifying the copyright monopoly. Overlooking this duality is how most misinterpret the Copyright Clause. Evidence of this can be found in an recent article on Techdirt.com titled *Fair Use, Public Domain And Creative Commons: They're Not All The Same* where the authors, Patricia Aufderheide and Peter Jaszi describe as a "badly eroded zone of copyright-free work." But, to the contrary, the public domain is as vibrant as ever. An extremely important component in the Constitutional construct is the fact the public benefits from the creation of the work not only when it enters the public domain, but *contemporaneously* at the time the work is published. Thus, the current emphasis on time limitations by opponents to the copyright monopoly is not well-placed, as it overlooks not only the many other existing checks and balances existing in current copyright law, as well as the dual benefit component in the construct of monopoly established by our Forefathers.

CHAPTER 10
Origins of an Idea:
Something New Under the Sun

When there is an original sound in the
World, it makes a hundred echoes.

-John Augustus Shedd

It was allegedly King Solomon who declared "there is nothing new under the sun!" Now a recent strain of thought seeks to recast King Solomon's casual and often misinterpreted observation in order to challenge the very basis of U.S. copyright laws, *i.e., challenge the existence of original ideas.* One of Falkvinge's seminal speeches during the formative years of The Pirate Party was titled "There is nothing new under the sun," a title for which, again no surprise, he gives no attribution to King Solomon but apparently uses for its weight of authority.

In that speech, Falkvinge asserts the concept of controlling ideas originates with the Roman Catholic Church and this idea "is undergoing a fundamental change today - because the

Internet does not follow the old model anymore. We not only download culture and knowledge. We upload it to others at the same time. We share files. The knowledge and the culture have amazingly lost their central point of control." Copyleft advocates are very focused on control.

This line of reasoning is followed and perhaps best exemplified in the popular Internet cult film by Brett Gaylor titled *RIP, A Remix Manifesto*, inspired by his need to defend the work of his favorite mash up artist, Gregg Gillis, professionally known as Girltalk. Girltalk achieved a level of success by taking the most prominent lyrics and melodic lines from sound recordings of popular songs from the 70's and beyond and "mashing them up" with other recordings. Girltalk's creations - called "genius" by some of his fans - often reproduce and manipulate dozens of sound recordings in a single song, thereby directly infringing the rights of dozens of owners of the sound recordings, as well as the owners of the musical composition.

Gaylor makes no bones about his attack on ideas, explaining to his audience near the beginning of the video it is "a film about the war of ideas, where the Internet is the battleground." So be it. Let's debate the film's primary cornerstone, the first and foundational clause of the Remix Manifesto, which is that "Culture always borrows from the past." Note that this is simply a rephrasing of that famous line attributed to King Solomon, "there is nothing new under the sun."

To be fair, the entire ReMix Manifesto set forth in Gaylor's film and certainly the ideology that undergirds it, is actually borrowed from Dr. Lawrence Lessig, who is a law professor at Stanford Law School. Lessig frequently lectures on copyright in the context of the remix phenomenon, using it to promote his own works which often seek to carve up the current copyright law into tiny pieces making it, in effect, useless. Lest you forget, however, Lessig's critical works are, in fact, registered for full copyright protection. Lessig develops the thesis of the ReMix Manifesto in his book, *Remix: Making Art & Commerce Thrive in the Hybrid Economy.* So, Lessig is prominently featured in the film and Gaylor does not shy away from his support of Lessig's thesis.

With that, an examination of Lessig's summary of King Solomon's premise - "culture always borrows from the past" - is in order. Without getting into the logical truth that drawing a universal conclusion from purely inductive reasoning is a fallacy (as Gaylor does in the film), such a universal assertion that culture always borrows from past *is, at best, probable, but most certainly indefinite.* It can be probable only if one can assume the truth of the premises used to support the conclusion, because the instant a person finds but one example of a contradicting premise – *i.e.,* in this case an example of something not borrowed from the past –the conclusion must be flawed.

Does such an example of something not borrowed from the past exist, or are King Solomon and Dr. Lessig correct? *To wit, is there no original thought?* I personally have a hard time accepting this premise. Spawning original ideas or creating an original thought, is, in my humble opinion, what separates us from other species, and truly defines us as unique.

The human species uses words, notes, colors, shapes, etc. as the building blocks of its ideas. As the early leaders of our nation envisioned, we draw inspiration from these components of the continuum of thought for the creation of new expressions. So, admittedly, in a broad sense we are using "the past" to create in some fundamental sense of that phrase. To be fair, this perhaps what King Solomon meant. But the fact that *building blocks* are used does not negate the possibility of an original thought, particularly when those are the means of communicating an idea, or of making it tangible.

There is an old postulation that if you put 50 monkeys in a room filled with typewriters, they are statistically incapable of replicating one of Shakespeare's sonnets simply by striking out random characters on the blank page. It is, in fact, statistically improbable the monkeys will even type out a string of words forming a cohesive thought. This anecdote illustrates the proposition that the mere existence of the building blocks of ideas does not negate original ideas, nor creative thought. If it did, the monkeys would be able to duplicate the Bard. But they cannot.

Something on the order of a "creative spark" is needed: one of those rare moments in human existence when a person reaches beyond his or her feeble, prosaic existence and grasps an original idea, a unique thought that, when expressed and made tangible, changes the course of human history. Immediately, names like Einstein, Mozart, Da Vinci and others come to mind. It's true this creative spark may not occur frequently, but it does happen.

Every now and again, albeit perhaps rare, we as humans have those sparks of an idea: something is invented or created – something original and unique – that changes, even if only in a small sense, the very nature of life for all humans who follow.

Granted, many of our great inventions and thoughts have been the amalgam of the collective thought of generations. But many still were built upon principles discovered hundreds of years prior. To that extent, the *broad* and *general* presumption that *most* of our ideas are built on the past may be true.

But it is not difficult to find, throughout the course of human history, original thoughts that propel us forward toward the destiny that is mankind's, affected forever by the new idea. What it must have been like to be around in the days when primitive humans began to formulate sounds, refining and defining until they developed a language, creating symbols, be it words or drawings, communicating their thoughts to another human being. What they must have felt when they developed the first rudimentary tools to perform the tasks necessary to sustain one's life in a hostile environment, fashioning a make-shift hammer with a rock, a reed, and a straight stick. These leaps in evolutionary development were not "borrowed" from the past, notwithstanding the fact they incorporated universal principles and building blocks. These were truly original expressions of thoughts.

Certainly, it can be said even these "inventions" were based on the gestures and functions necessary to communicate or strike an animal to sustain life, but that is a far cry from saying the invention of the screwdriver - or even the screw - was based on the prior idea of using our fingers to turn an object. There is a vast difference between gesturing at one's mouth to indicate hunger, and forming a collection of sounds and symbols which, when communicated, means "let's get lunch." The latter is not built on the past in any real sense.

In the film, Gaylor makes the point Gutenberg's invention of the printing press occurred during a time when the public domain flourished. His use of this example is, in this case, ironic, since the printing press can, in my mind, truly be defined as one of those creative bursts of unique ideas that only come along one is a few millennia. Since that invention, perhaps only the creation of the Internet has affected the world as much as Gutenberg's original thought. Yes, long prior to Gutenberg there were means of producing written communications. I'm certain some mother somewhere had previously showed her son how to carve a potato, dip it in ink, and press it onto fabric or material and create duplicates of the "communication. Do these prior existing technologies mean Gutenberg borrowed from the past? In the strictest sense, of course they do. But if you step back and look at the original thought that took Gutenberg from where society was at the time to the giant leap forward he produced, there is no doubt his invention was, in fact, something new under the sun. To say his idea "borrowed from the past" in any real sense truly diminishes the magnitude of his work. His was an original idea.

Rather than describing them as "borrowing from the past," it is better to think of inventors like Gutenberg as weaving new threads into the tapestry of the human continuum. The new threads may "cast on" existing threads of thought, but they take the patterns of humanity in entirely unique and new directions. This is the impact of original thought.

Proponents of the argument culture always borrows from the past often point to the invention of the light bulb as an example bolstering their defense: even though Thomas Edison is given credit for inventing the light bulb, they maintain other inventors such as Joseph Swan and Edward Wesson were working on the incandescent bulb in the same time frame. But the fact *several persons* have a similar, yet no less original, idea does not negate its originality. The idea of an *electric* bulb is original, regardless the number of humans working on the concept. More importantly, the idea of a constant light source did not, in anything but a remotely vague sense of illumination, borrow from the idea of a candle's flame. The electric light bulb did not borrow from the past. The electric light bulb *was*, perhaps ironically, something new "under the sun."

Any discussion of original ideas in science would not be complete without referencing the geniuses of Isaac Newton and Albert Einstein. When Newton first considered the acceleration of moving bodies, he begin to form the foundation for his invention of the mathematical tools of calculus, a field of mathematics not existing prior to Newton, *i.e.*, it was an original field of thought. While Newton may have woven his threads into the existing field of mathematics, he did not borrow from them. Stated more directly, the fact mathematics existed as a field of study does not negate the fact calculus was an original idea. Newton incorporated universal principles of mathematics, indeed, but his original thought was expressed in the form of something new, *i.e.* calculus. In this case, again, there was something new under the sun.

The field of physics also produces several great examples of original thinkers, of which everyone's favorite genius, Albert Einstein, is perhaps the most colorful and insightful. Einstein reached up out of the human plane and grasped a spark of originality when he compared the similarity between gravity and an accelerating spaceship, a thought which led him to discover one of the most significant theories of the 20th century: the general theory of relativity. He described it the "happiest thought of my life." This is perhaps the pinnacle of original thought and is certainly a glimpse at the human response to it. We will explore this in more detail in the next chapter.

Coming in a close second to Einstein's theory of relativity is the second example from the field of physics: Schrodinger's idea to formulate quantum mechanics using his wave equation. Prior influences on the lives of Einstein and Schrodinger notwithstanding, relativity and quantum theory are original thoughts: they cannot, in any relevant manner, be accurately described as "borrowing from the past." These ideas were one of a kind, unique and original: changing the paradigms of the past and thus forever altering the thinking of subsequent generations.

Only in the most general of senses can one seriously maintain these remarkably useful and unique ideas sustain the principle "culture always borrows from the past." There was, at the time, nothing like them under the sun. These are but a few examples of those brilliant moments in human history when someone has that flash of an original idea and created something uniquely and totally new, something that does not, in any substantive sense, borrow from the past. Whether you believe these moments are inspired by deity, infused by a muse, induced by hallucinogenic means, or just a nightmare inspired by a bout of angina, the fact is, at least in that moment, we are witness to the origins of an idea.

After initially resisting the institution of a monopoly for intellectual creations, Jefferson later caught a glimpse of the benefits in his new Republic. In a letter to Benjamin Vaughn written in 1790, he confessed:

> An Act of Congress authorizing the issuing of patents for new discoveries has given a spring of invention beyond my conception. . . . Many of them indeed are trifling, but there are some of great consequence which have been proved by practice, and others which if they stand the same proof *will produce a great effect.*

As introduced elsewhere, Jefferson was the most qualified of our Forefathers to understand the origins of an idea, as he was an avid inventor and thinker. Among his many inventions identified earlier, the notable invention of the wheel cipher serves as a good example. While serving as the Secretary of State in the early 1790's, the Washington administration was faced with national security issues. Jefferson had a flash of original insight. He set about to solve the problem by creating a device which consisted of twenty-six cylindrical wooden pieces with the letters of the alphabet inscribed on the edge. Each cylinder had a hole bored into the center so it could be threaded onto an iron spindle in unison with the other 25. By rotating the wheels of the cipher, a person could scramble and unscramble messages encoded with the same series. Original thought is often most fertile when necessity creates a void.

I offer these illustrations to point out that abolishing the concept of original thought is not the foundation upon which we as a society should build a debate against the current construct of copyright law. While the implementation may be in need of reform, the principles must remain steadfast. We should cling to the concept of original thought, for it is in that moment, *i.e., that origin of an original idea*, when humans *distinguish* themselves from the past, not borrow from it. It is at that moment our culture is propelled into the future - sometimes, as in the cases of Gutenberg, Newton and Schrodinger, decades into the future. It is at that moment of original thought, I believe, we are truly alive - truly "God-like," if you will. In that moment, original thoughts are born again.

CHAPTER 11

Original Thought

The more intelligent one is,
the more men of originality one finds.
Ordinary people find no difference between men.

-Blaise Pascal

The most beautiful thing we can experience is the mysterious.
It is the source of all true art and science.

— Albert Einstein

If the more intelligent among us can find original thought, as Pascal says in the quote above, the question of the day becomes *what is original thought?* Is it capable of our understanding or is it, as Einstein alludes, too mysterious for the ordinary man? In other words, in order to answer the question of whether original thought can still exist, we must first define the phrase.

For me, I can only begin to grasp the concept of original thought when I consider further the life and context that generated the words of Albert Einstein:

> A new idea comes suddenly and in a rather intuitive way.
> That means it is not reached by conscious logical conclusions.
> But, thinking it through afterwards, you can always discover
> the reasons which have led you unconsciously to your guess
> and you will find a logical way to justify it. Intuition is
> nothing but the outcome of earlier intellectual experience.

This quotation from the mind of Einstein brings to mind one of
my favorite witticisms, the suggestion that a person "put that in
his pipe and smoke it," meaning to "sleep on it "or give it careful
consideration. This perhaps trivializes the important observation
made by Einstein here, *it is our intellectual experience that
provides the unconscious fertilizer for original thought.* Einstein
once said "truth is independent of our consciousness. . . ." What
we can learn from this is that original thought de-emphasizes
"logic" and emphasizes intuition. Perhaps this is the mystery to
which Einstein referred in the earlier quotation.

As much as we may be identical on the molecular level of
DNA encoding, each person is made up of unique and individual
experiences that formulate the "sieve" through which they filter
perceptions. This was just as true of Thomas Jefferson as it was
true of Albert Einstein. No one escapes the millions of mundane
aspects of everyday life that must be attended to, all of which
impact a person's unique world view. Unique world views are
the primordial soup out of which original ideas crawl and evolve
into thoughts, ultimately leading to the mutation known as
innovation.

This theory calls into question the one expressed by Edwin
C. Hettinger in his article "Justifying Intellectual Property," who
argued intellectual creations do not exist in a vacuum, but rather
are "social products." Any intellectual work is built on the prior

work of numerous people and original thought is therefore inconceivable. Hettinger's conclusion is similar in concept to Lessig's "culture always borrows from the past," as addressed in the previous chapter. Original thoughts may arise from an individual's unique experience in society, but all inventions are *not, a posteriori,* social ideas.

To the degree original thought does in fact arise from unique experiences, as I propose, the concept of *thought* might be distinguishable from the concept of *ideas.* Ideas may be thought of as something common to everyone. Thought, on the other hand, is a person's unique perception and interpretation of that idea, as conceived wholly in their brains and known only to them. It is this Jefferson referred to in his famous letter to McPherson when he stated:

> If nature has made any one thing less susceptible than all others to exclusive property, it is the action of the thinking power called an idea, which an individual may exclusively possess as long as he keeps it to himself; but the moment it is divulged, it focuses itself into the possession of every one, and the receiver cannot dispossess himself of it. Its peculiar character, too, is that no one possesses the less because every other possesses the whole of it. He who receives an idea from me, receives instruction himself without lessening mine; as he who lights his taper at mine, receives light without darkening me.

At the risk of correcting one of the greatest thinkers of all time, if my distinction is accurate, what Jefferson is referring to here when he uses the word *idea* is perhaps better characterizes as a *thought.* An idea, such as the idea of a rock, for example, actually exists in nature regardless of whether we perceive it or not. Whether the *idea* of the rock exists independently of its actual existence, as Plato maintained in his concept of duality, is irrelevant to our discussion. The physical existence of the rock, and with it the connected theoretical idea thereof, existed prior to my existence and will prevail long after I am dead and gone. But my individual thoughts about rocks are uniquely mine and if they remain in my brain without revelation to a third party, will die along with me. They are uniquely mine.

These thoughts germinate in our minds until they are expressed through innovation, as illustrated in the diagram below:

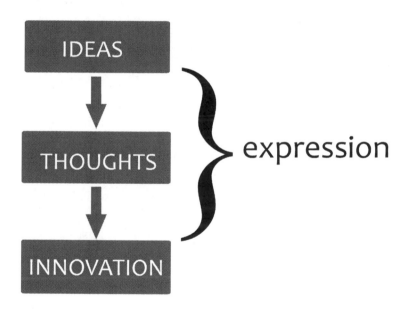

Reflect on this flow from ideas to thoughts to innovation in the context of an earlier point in the discussion, the example of Einstein. He thought about the ideas of gravity and speed. He considered mass and energy. But a myriad of other researchers and scientists, like Leibniz, also thought about these concepts. Einstein certainly was not the only person thinking about these ideas. Gravity and speed are components of the continuum of thought from which any creator and inventor may draw for inspiration. But Einstein's thought was the only thought in history that ultimately spawned the innovation he ultimately expressed and perhaps his was the only experience in history that could ever have produced it. Einstein's ideas about speed and gravity germinated thoughts, which led to an innovation ultimately becoming reality.

What, then, makes Einstein's thoughts about these ideas original thought? Consider the fact Einstein did not think about these things in the confines of an "ivory tower" intellectual environment. As a very young child, Albert contemplated his father's compass and was fascinated with the idea there was some invisible force moving the needle around the face. As a young adult, Einstein was relegated to thinking his thoughts about electromagnetism while a student at Polytechnic at Zurich while, like many of us, he was suffering through the financial difficulties of trying to support his family while getting an education at the same time. These thoughts brewed alongside his frustrations of being passed over for an academic post, like most others in his section received. They were in the back of his mind when his failure to obtain a teaching position forcing him to ask his father to persuade a friend at the Swiss Patent Office to give him a job. While there, his father died and he married his then-fiancée against his families' wishes, and had a child, both of whom he had to support on a meager salary. All the while, his spare time was spent pursing his doctorate at the University of Zurich and he would take every opportunity he could to join weekly discussion groups talking about science and philosophy. Perhaps, these perceptions of ideas were swirling in his head simultaneously with the hurt he must have felt watching his mother being forced to take a job housecleaning after his father died.

All these forces impacted the thoughts Einstein generated, unconsciously, as he went about his daily tasks. He described them as "the irrational, the inconsistent, the droll, even the insane, which nature, inexhaustibly operative, implants into the individual, seemingly for her own amusement." Each individual, genius or not, experiences the droll. These are the elements of the creative process. These are the ingredients in the soup of life that is sparked and evolves into the origins of a thought, the unique and original thought only a thinking person can generate. It evolves from an idea, not entitled to protection as intellectual property, into a thought, and finally into to innovation. There is a point along that evolutionary scale at which the process becomes an expression of the thought and, once fixed, becomes a copyright. For Einstein, it led in 1905 to the publication of the four scientific papers known as his *Annus Mirabilis* papers, including the one on special relativity and the mass-energy equivalence.

Now, perhaps one will jump ahead and say Einstein may very well have been familiar with the earlier work of the German, Gottfried Leibniz, mentioned earlier, who years before Einstein contemplated the relationship between mass and energy and derived an equation uncannily similar to Einstein's, that being $e=mv2$, or energy equals the motion of all masses multiplied by their respective velocities squared. Notwithstanding its similarity, however, the existence of the Leibniz formula does not negate the originality of Einstein's.

As Eric Hoffer explains:

> Perhaps our originality manifests itself most strikingly in what we do with that which we did not originate. To discover something wholly new can be a matter of chance, of idle tinkering, or even of the chronic dissatisfaction of the untalented.

One thing is certain: Einstein was not untalented, and likely his was not a chance event. As Einstein lived his life, his beautiful mind churned through his thoughts about the ideas already present around him and generated the original idea that grew into the innovation expressed as the special theory of relativity and the mass-energy equivalence, the latter being the most unique insight Einstein provided: his realization that matter and energy are really different forms of the same thing. Matter can be turned into energy and, conversely, energy into matter. Even if his famous equation, e=mc2, were proven to be false as some scientists now claim may be possible, his contribution would be no less original. In that sense, Einstein's was not an incremental improvement to an already existing idea. His was not "borrowing from the past." As he described it, his idea came suddenly and was the "outcome of earlier intellectual experience." His absolutely was not a social product. His innovation was original.

What characterizes the original thought of such geniuses as Einstein? Some researchers today, like Hal Gregersen at INSEAD and Jeffrey Dyer at BYU, and Clayton Christensen at Harvard belief something called "associated thinking" is at the heart of innovation, that being the ability to make connections between seemingly unconnected things. The original thinker knows that there are numerous solutions to any problem. This is perhaps the DNA of original thought.

Einstein once said of his own inquiries,

> The important thing is not to stop questioning; curiosity has its own reason for existing. One cannot help but be in awe when contemplating the mysteries of eternity, of life, of the marvelous structure of reality. It is enough if one tries merely to comprehend a little of the mystery every day. The important thing is not to stop questioning; never lose a holy curiosity.

Einstein is telling us here the origins of an idea are shrouded in the mysteries of eternity and life, but that they are very real and comprehensible if we take the time to think. It is probable no other mind in history, before or since, could have generated the original thought Einstein gave us. Since being published, Einstein's original idea has done more for the advancement of physics than any other thought in history.

But deriving my example of original thought from the annals of science may be viewed as disingenuous to some if applied to the creative arts, such as music or literature, where it is not difficult to see new lines of thinking. Surely, many would argue, such originality cannot be found in creation of music utilizing a scale containing a mere 7 notes, only 8 octaves of which are perceptible by most human ears.

In order to understand original thought in music, one again must consider the difference between the idea, in this case the note, and the thought as the latter germinates into a final innovation. Each person brings to a musical thought a different set of filters which serve to color the end product which is, in many instances, an original idea or thought. If that supposition is true, then an original thought regarding a musical composition is no less unique than Einstein's thoughts regarding relativity, albeit perhaps much less impactful on the course of human history. It follows the same pathway, receiving inspiration in common ideas, developing into a cohesive thought filtered through experience and finally expressing itself in an innovation.

The originality of thought in music is ironically illustrated by examining an example used in the film mentioned earlier, *RIP: A Remix Manifesto,* to persuade the viewer GirlTalk's music is creative. In it, Gaylor plays a sample of the guitar segue between Queen's *We Will Rock You* and *We are the Champions,* as used by his favorite artist GirlTalk in one of his mash-up songs. To set up the red herring, he coaxes the viewer to identify the writer of the song, and then states that if you guessed "Queen," you are wrong. Why, you might ask? Gaylor explains:

> Because this music was created by my favorite artist, Girl Talk. Girl Talk makes mash ups. His computer is an instrument. . . and the notes he plays are sampled from thousands of pop music classics, cut up and rearranged to create new songs.

In this one statement lays the crux of our contemporary problem. Using a sample of an original sound recording to create a derived work does not a creator make. It voids the process of originality. Further, it ignores the distinction between the creator of the musical composition and the creator of the sound recording itself, each individual works of original art under current copyright law.

161

To further complicate issues, Gaylor concludes his diatribe with the following syllogism, which is the heart of his video:

The rules of this game don't depend on who made the song.
The rules of the game depend on who owns the copyright.

Now, any first year copyright law student can tell you that in the world of musical compositions, the person *who made the song* is the same person *who owns the copyright*, at least unless and until that copyright is transferred. Realizing that these two phrases are essentially the same, we designate both second terms of the premises as "B." We designate the first terms of Gaylor's premises, "the rules of the game," as "A." Applying basic principal of logics, Gaylor's syllogism is therefore shown to be false: A≠B, so A=B. Stated this way, the fallacy is obvious.

This digression into the details of logic is not intended merely to prove the logical fallacies of Gaylor's arguments as such, but more importantly to illustrate there is an original thought imbedded in the sound recording GirlTalk uses to "create" something Gaylor considers new. The point is the true originality in the creation of this music is misplaced.

The musical segue between Queen's *We Will Rock You* and *We are the Champions* was actually created by Brian May, now Doctor Brian May. The original thought belonged to him and was expressed through his sieve of experience and response. On April 3, 2010, he appeared on NPR's *Fresh Air* program discussing the solo. Here is what Dr. May describes as the intellectual process of thought leading to his spark of creativity:

The guitar - yeah, I didn't want us to be standard. I didn't want it to be like oh, here's a guitar solo, and then we sing another verse. I wanted it to be something stark and different. So it was very deliberate that I left the guitar solo to the end because that was a final statement and a different statement, taking it off in a completely different direction. It changes key into that piece, too, you know, so it's a whole different kind of shape. It was not a standard pop song.

You can hear the guitar waiting in the wings. You can hear this little feedback note. And so the guitar is present, although it's not taking center stage, all through the last choruses, and then finally, it bursts upon the scene.

And you notice, Freddie goes "all right," which means he's kind of handing over to the guitar, and we're in a different universe once the guitar starts, and that was the intention. And it's very sort of informal.

. . .You may notice that the last piece, the very last little riffs, are repeated, and they're not just repeated by me playing them again. They're repeated by cutting the tape and splicing it on again and again.

So - and that's deliberate, too. It's a way of getting a sort of a thing that makes you sit up towards the end. And then it stops. There is nothing after it, which I really enjoy!

Arising out of Dr. May's unique experiences, originality is inspired by an idea that developed into his own unique thoughts. The thoughts manifested themselves through innovation. Dr. May was creating an original musical segue unlike any other expression occurring before it. It is an expression still unique in the world of musical compositions. Other writers, of course, have written guitar solos. Other writers have "layered" riffs on top of identical riffs to create effect. These are examples of the ideas that exist in the continuum of thought. But Dr. May's ultimate expression of these ideas turned into thoughts was uniquely his. It was original thought. At that moment in history, Dr. May drew from his subconscious, lifted his hand out of the pool of the mundane and the droll, and grabbed an original thought. It is rare, but it is not impossible.

The evolution from idea to thought to innovation may best be illustrated by two art forms that, under our current Copyright Act of 1976, are entitled to protection: choreography and pantomime. Both of these art forms, in their simplest state of existence, border on pure ideas. The Copyright Office made it clear, however, their entitlement to copyright protection does not depend upon them telling a story, but only require a modicum of originality in order to gain the monopoly. Think of a pantomime artist performing the "man in a box" routine. That simple act is very close to being mere idea, perhaps not entitled to copyright protection. But combine it with additional maneuvers and gestures and the form resembling an idea starts to take shape as a thought, and then rises out of the fire as an innovation. The more the idea takes on the clothing of expressed thought, the more it becomes an original creation entitled to copyright protection.

Returning once again to the world of pop music for illustration of this evolution from idea to a protected monopoly. Fans of Paul Simon will know that the famous drummer, Steve Gadds, played the initial drum riff that continues throughout the song titled *Fifty Ways to Leave Your Lover*. If you listen to that drum riff in isolation from the song, it can be dissected to the point it is merely quarter notes mixed with sixteenth notes in syncopated time sequence. But include the emphasis on the licks created by the mind of Gadds and build around it the lyrics and melody as they develop, and the original expression begins to take shape, again arising out of the continuum of ideas. That particular rhythm is so unique it literally integrates with the other components to give the song a original feel. While rhythm, by itself, is typically not granted copyright protection, this example might just qualify.

Giorgio Vasari may have best summed up this idea of an individual mind's contribution to original thought in his 1568 work, *Lives of the Artists*, in which he described Leonardo da Vinci as follows:

> In the normal course of events many men and women are born with remarkable talents; but occasionally, in a way that transcends nature, a single person is marvelously endowed by Heaven with beauty, grace and talent in such abundance that he leaves other men far behind, all his actions seem inspired and indeed everything he does clearly comes from God rather than from human skill. Everyone acknowledged that this was true of Leonardo da Vinci, an artist of outstanding physical beauty, who displayed infinite grace in everything that he did and who cultivated his genius so brilliantly that all problems he studied he solved with ease.

Dr. May and Steve Gadds would likely not compare themselves to da Vinci, but in the moment May first gestated this idea into a thought that turned into an innovative guitar riff, Dr. May experienced the origins of an idea that forever affected the course of pop music. Likewise, when Gadds first incorporated his unique rhythmic patterns to the collage of ideas that evolved into *Fifty Ways to Leave Your Lover*, he was affecting the course of music and experiencing the origins of an idea. Yes, their original threads wove themselves into the tapestry of a continuum of thoughts some of which stretched back for several centuries, *i.e.*, existing chords, notes, techniques, genres, etc. But as I have stated before, using the existing

Zeitgeist does not negate the possibility of originality when it is filtered through the individual mind of the creative.

Now, while we admit Dr. May and Mr. Gadds are perhaps not on the level of a da Vinci and we can certainly not ignore the fact the impact of their unique ideas on the field of music is perhaps not as great as the impact Einstein's theory of special relativity has on the world of physics, this admission does not diminish the uniqueness and originality of their expressed ideas.

It is perhaps for this reason our U.S. Copyright laws do not require uniqueness of an idea in order to grant the monopoly of copyright, but rather requires only what the Supreme Court has described as a *modicum of originality.* As such, in the creative arts, the level of original thought does not have to rise to the same level of uniqueness required under patent law.

If the antagonists were to have their desired goal of eliminating copyright as we know it, what would become of original thought as I have described it? In the film, Gaylor says the recording of Dr. May's guitar solo is one of the "notes" used by GirlTalk to "create" his music, and the computer is his instrument. But such equivocation is a self-fulfilling prophecy. The end of copyright, or more precisely the end of original thought, means creativity degenerates into mash-ups of previously recorded material. Is that the kind of world we want?

Original thought and innovation are easily distinguishable from the collage of sound recordings found in mash-ups created by "artists" like GirlTalk. As Mary Beth Peters, then Register of Copyrights, humbly concluded in her interview vignette in Gaylor's film, "One cannot claim creativity in other people's creation." That is precisely the point. Ultimately, creative innovation is derived from one's original thoughts about universal ideas, not by combining a variety of other people's original thoughts and claiming them as your own. This is the essence of copyright law.

In final analysis, it is sometimes difficult to distinguish between an idea and a thought. Thought is most appropriately defined in the context of an individual's mental activity, whether conscious or unconscious, whereas ideas are dependent upon social and linguistic structures, rather than the self-standing creations of an individual mind. This is why, in my construct, the idea is the inspiration for original thought. Ideas are part of human culture, whereas thoughts can be individualized.

The concept of *ideation* incorporates both concepts and provides the transition from ideas to thoughts. Assumedly the two never intermingle, but rather ideas may "bleed into" thoughts. This is where the confusion between the two concepts often arises. Thoughts are often combined to form concepts in the mind, so in this sense can still be maintained inside a person's head without revealing them. The distinction to be drawn is the concept of an "idea" should be confined to the continuum of societal knowledge, not the individual mind, which is the fertile playground of original thoughts. For this reason, it may be better to refer to these as *archetypal* ideas, as did Plato.

So, in the context of creativity and original thought, it is a useful construct to keep the two concepts of archetypal ideas and individualized original thought separate. Archetypal ideas exist in the Zeitgeist, in what we've referred to as the continuum of knowledge. Archetype ideas belong to everyone and cannot be subjected to a monopoly. Thoughts, on the other hand, are the products of our individual minds inspired by archetypal ideas, which are both processed through our experiential world view. Through the process of ideation, these thoughts are often expressed in unique and original constructs. The original thoughts, once expressed, become subject to the application of the copyright monopoly.

CHAPTER 12

And yet it Moves

Do not believe in traditions
because they have been handed down for many generations.
But after observation and analysis,
when you find that anything agrees with reason
and is conducive to the good and benefit of one and all,
then accept it and live up to it.

-Gautama Siddharta

There is, as I have previously mentioned, a prevailing ideology that maintains we are living at a time when every original idea has been exhausted. Similar to the recent lyric of *You Never* Know by the contemporary band Wilco states, "every generation thinks it's the last, thinks it's the end of the world." This extreme position resembles the arrogance of almost every powerful society in history that has falsely believed theirs is the most prolific and, therefore, the last great society.

During Isaac Newton's lifetime, there were so many predictions of when his generation would end that in a manuscript written in 1704, he extracted "scientific information" from the Bible to estimate the world would end no earlier than 2060. Newton did this not so much to throw his hat in the ring with an offer of his own prediction about the precise time the world would end, but rather to dissuade belief in the other less generous predications which held the world as they knew it would soon end. He explained:

> This I mention not to assert when the time of the end shall be, but to put a stop to the rash conjectures of fanciful men who are frequently predicting the time of the end, and by doing so bring the sacred prophesies into discredit as often as their predictions fail.

Such predictions of end times need not be based in religious thought and more frequently than not are simply a product of every successful generation. For example, the South American Inca Empire was the largest empire from the early 1400's until its demise at the hand of Spaniards in 1572. The Inca's were a prolifically creative culture, developing original thought in the area of impressive architecture, language, and even surgical techniques. It is almost a given many in the Incan world would have felt theirs was the most prolific society ever to exist and all original ideas were conceived by their culture. The benefit of hindsight has taught us, however, that they were not the last great society, nor were they the first. As prolific as their society may have been, it did not exhaust original thought.

Over a thousand years prior to the Incan Empire, the Roman Empire was another equally prolific great society. The Roman Empire existed for over 500 years and during that time exhausted its creative efforts by producing a wealth of literature, theater, sculpture, architecture, languages, and religions. Some scholars estimate it had a total gross national product equivalent to over $43 billion in current U.S. dollars. The Roman Empire effectively came to an end when the government of Constantinople began installing emperors in the mid 400's. But the Roman Empire did not exhaust original thought any more than societies prior to its existence.

Ostensibly prior to all this, the writer of Ecclesiastes is credited with the saying quoted earlier, "What has been will be again, what has been done will be done again; there is nothing new under the sun." Perhaps the writer was referring to the Ancient Egyptian civilization that coalesced around 3150 B.C.E. in Northeastern Africa, one of modern society's earliest successful cultures. The Egyptians left their creative mark in the form of pyramids that, in so many respects, remain an enigma to modern engineering to this day. In addition to these monuments, the Egyptians are also credited with creating an original alphabetical language, as well as a new system of mathematics, effective new medical techniques, new glass technology, agricultural production and irrigation techniques, as well as the first known ships. The ancient Egyptians were a very productive and sophisticated people who left a lasting legacy, yet they were not the last to have original thoughts and express them in prolific and profound ways. Alas, this culture fell to the Roman Empire in 30 B.C.E., long before original thought expired.

The perplexing philosophy that the most current and recent generation is so prolific as to possibly exhaust original thought is a mere corollary to this arrogantly false idea that every great nation in history was the last great society: when our society dies, so too does original thought. Our current society and culture, as great as it is, is not the last society. We are an extremely prolific generation but, our current society, no matter how prolific, has not exhausted all original thought. Faced with examples from history such as the Incan, Roman, and Egyptian societies, such a proposition is arrogance personified. It is an affront to past generations that produced original thought and it is a slap in the face to generations certain to exist thousands of years from now, generations that will undoubtedly be great and produce a wealth of original thought. Rest assured the continuum of thought flowed through all these great societies and will continue to flood into future generations.

The reasons a culture develops the grandiose idea theirs is the pinnacle of all historical achievement extend beyond the scope of this analysis. The human desire to be remembered beyond the time of our ultimate demise is, of course, one of the most compelling rationales. But we as a society cannot allow those who fear the unknown to erase a well-conceived and finely tuned copyright construct that has served us well for hundreds of years simply because they believe no new thought is possible. New thought arises in every society and what we do in this culture will not affect that historical fact: the Egyptians built the pyramids and gave us language and mathematics; the Romans gave the world the aqueducts and early forms of Christianity; the Chinese gave the world the great wall; the Mayan civilization produced the first fully developed written language of the Americas, as well as a system of mathematics and astronomy. Our culture has produced many great technological advances catapulting us light-years ahead of those impressive societies, yet there is more original thought to be discovered. The truth is all previous advances were mere drops in the river making up the flow of the continuum of thought. There are future generations whose innovations will contribute in ways we cannot currently conceive.

As Shakespeare's Hamlet proclaims to Horatio in Act 1, "There are more things in heaven and earth . . . than are dreamt of in your philosophy." The more we as a society focus solely on incorporating the past, as in "culture always borrows from the past," the more we suppress original thought.

It is good for society that Galileo Galilei did not suppress his original thought of heliocentrism, *i.e.*, the earth revolves around the sun, in complete isolation of the prevailing thought of his and prior cultures, *i.e.*, the sun rotates around the earth. Perhaps his contemporaries were also convinced no original thought regarding the subject was possible. Galileo's idea was so controversial because it was ostensibly contrary to the teachings of the Bible. His thought was so novel it landed him in a trial in front of the Roman Inquisition in 1633, where he was found "vehemently suspect of heresy." After being forced to recant his original thought, legend has it Galileo muttered the words "and yet it moves" under his breathe, in defiant reference, of course, to the movement of the earth.

The same could be said for original thought: and yet it moves, despite those around us who say otherwise. Thankfully, in the United States at least, we live in a culture that embraces original thought, at least for now. It sobers me to think otherwise. As Isaac Newton contemplated in one of his last memoirs:

> I do not know what I may appear to the world, but to myself I seem to have been only like a boy playing on the sea-shore, and diverting myself in now and then finding a smoother pebble or a prettier shell than ordinary, whilst the great ocean of truth lay all undiscovered before me.

There is great ocean of original thought before us. Let us not focus on the pretty shells of past cultures laying on the shores while its undiscovered waves pound at our feet.

CHAPTER 13

Through the Looking Glass

*"We can't solve problems by using the same kind of thinking
we used when we created them."*

-Albert Einstein

*"Somehow it seems to fill my head with ideas —
only I don't exactly know what they are!"*

-Lewis Carroll
Through the Looking Glass

The copyright construct works precisely because of the flexibility our Forefathers built into the Constitution. Digital technology has not destroyed the construct conceived by Madison, Pinckney, Jefferson, and the founding delegates attending the Constitution Convention.

In his work *Economy of Ideas*, however, John Perry Barlow maintains "Digital technology is detaching information from the physical plane, where property law of all sorts has found definition." But is that a true statement?

Yes, technology has altered how we *perceive* our original thoughts. We no longer use physical objects like paper and plastic to embody the original expression; rather, the expression is conveyed in machine readable code. Nothing has changed: when the code is processed by the machine, the original thought is expressed, whether that be through an earphone attached to an iPhone or a monitor attached to a computer or some other electronic device. So long as original thought can be expressed, it can be monopolized. End of story.

Incidentally, as discussed previously, the idea of owning property, *i.e.* property law, is no more defined in the "physical plane" Barlow describes than is intellectual property ownership. As previously illustrated, both are legal fictions created by society. The first is equally as ephemeral as the latter.

That Barlow misses this point is evident in this question from *Economy of Ideas:*

> Thus the rights of invention and authorship adhered to activities in the physical world. One didn't get paid for ideas but for the ability to deliver them into reality. For all practical purposes, the value was in the conveyance and not the thought conveyed.

If Barlow's conclusion here is true, the word *conveyance* must be understood as a synonym for *expression*. I emphatically deny, however, that Barlow's conclusion is true. Yes, expression is necessary to receive protection of one's copyright. No doubt, it must be expressed in a format perceivable for more than a limited time. Recognizing this important element of copyright should not de-emphasize the equally important component of original thought. As we saw in an earlier chapter, original thought is where the dividing line between a bare idea and an innovative thought starts to materialize. The focus should not be placed on the archetypal idea, but rather on the original thought filtered through the creator's own unique experience. It is, in fact, that original thought in which the creator is entitled to exercise the copyright monopoly.

Procedurally, yes, there has to be an expression in order to enforce the original thought. By law, the expression has to be a definable, tangible format. The original thought has to be conveyed as such in order to receive the monopoly. But it is the original thought converted into innovation that generates the entitlement, not the mere expression of it. The latter is best thought of as a formality. That is the conundrum our Founding Fathers grabbled with and for which they achieved a remarkably valid solution, one which I believe, contrary to Barlow and others, still functions well even in our modern age of digitization.

So how do we slow this prevailing tide in our current culture against the remarkable gift of our Founding Father called copyright? One obvious solution would be to reclaim the philosophy of our Founding Fathers. By that, I mean our Founding Fathers believed, according to nature, a person should be entitled to receive the "fruits of their labor." Whether that labor is applied to real property, as in tilling the soil to grow a garden, or applied to musical notes, as in writing an original composition. This was, for them, the "natural law" component of the copyright construct. But the real motivation for providing their new citizens with a copyright monopoly backed by the government was to serve the more utilitarian purpose of creating a free flowing market place of ideas which would inspire its citizens to create new and original thoughts. It is this perpetual cycle of inspiration, ideation, and innovation that was envisioned by our Founders and it is this to which we should aspire.

I said in the beginning I was, to some degree, returning to my theological training in an effort to defend the construct of copyright and to that extent there is a level of idealism in my arguments. One writer that, perhaps, had the most influence on my thinking during my studies in that regard was C.S. Lewis. In his seminal work, *Mere Christianity*, in the context of natural law, Lewis maintained that everyone routinely appealed "to some kind of standard of behavior which he expects the other man to know about" in the context of common quarrels about common notions of fairness. One example from our current Zeitgeist is the right to call "shot gun" which, in current nomenclature, means the first person to shout this phrase when approaching a vehicle gets to ride in the front passenger seat. But there is no written law or rule to this effect, it merely is. This, Lewis says, is a remnant of "natural law." He says:

> Quarreling means trying to show that the other man is in the wrong. And there would be no sense in trying to do that unless you and he had some sort of agreement as to what Right and Wrong are; just as there would be no sense in saying that a footballer had committed a foul unless there was some agreement about the rules of football.

Unlike the example of "shot gun" the rules of football are, in Lewis' example, written down, much like the rules of copyright in our society. At some point in our cultures' recent past, our representatives assembled and came to an agreement about the "rules" of copyright, and decided what was right and wrong with regard to it. As such, as much as copyright antagonists such as Falkvinge would have us believe otherwise, the prominent and prevailing view in our society is that incorporating someone's original thought as your own is wrong. Whether you call it plagiarism, pirating, theft, or infringement matters not, as all are just synonyms for that which we all know, from our sense of fairness, to be wrong.

Now, this argument is conceived in natural law and it is important to remember our copyright construct was not based on natural law, but rather utilitarianism. Yes, natural law was a prevalent part of thinking in early America and it most certainly had a dramatic impact on the perceptions of our Founding Fathers. Remnants of natural law philosophies can still be found in an analysis of many of our founding documents. But we must remember that Locke, although a natural law proponent, in the end looked more like a utilitarian because he believed only through an application of utilitarianism could you achieve a proper expression of natural law. In other word, to appease our sense of right and wrong, *i.e.*, our natural law, we had to form a society that protected the interests and rights of the many, *i.e.*, form a utilitarian government. The copyright monopoly concept is the best example of where Locke's view most profoundly impacted our Founding Fathers' thinking and sneaked its way into our laws through the pens of Madison, Jefferson, and others.

Most people who download an MP3 from the Internet without compensating the creator of the musical composition or the creator of the sound recording likely feel the tug between right and wrong. There is a voice inside their heads telling them someone is not getting treated fairly. Even those who claim what they do it as a form of rebellion against what they perceive as the greedy content industry that controls everything and steal from the artists anyway are merely using this as a justification.

I would even go so far as to speculate the likes of Falkvinge realize their position is a mere response to this impulse to justify their actions. If they did not feel in their subconscious mind it was wrong, why would any justification be necessary? If they would only listen to what Freud described as the dynamic unconscious, natural law would likely teach it is wrong. These feelings can only be suppressed, they cannot be eliminated. As C.S. Lewis said:

> Whenever you find a man who says he does not believe in a real Right and Wrong, you will find the same man going back on this a moment later. He may break his promise to you, but if you try breaking one to him he will be complaining "It's not fair. . . ."

Ever since the days of Plato and Aristotle, philosophers have attempted to divine a theory of what keeps society from deteriorating into chaos and anarchy, a state Thomas Hobbes later called the "war of all against all." The answer usually involves some variation of this innate sense of justice to which Lewis is referring. This is why the chapter discussing the *Ring of Gyges* is so crucial. The moral of that story, according to Plato, was that good people listen to their internal voice and pay attention the call of nature, the call of justice and fairness. Even in situations of anonymity, this person who will feel drawn to the natural law and will do what is just and fair. As the Boise student quoted in that chapter proclaimed: "I don't do it because I don't feel it's right. If I were making the music, I'd be upset if people were downloading it for free." In other words, she decided to abstain from stealing music because it offended her sense of right and wrong.

But Lewis made another interesting point in his discussion of natural law and our adherence to it:

Each man is at every moment subjected to several different sets of law but there is only one of these which he is free to disobey. As a body, he is subjected to gravitation and cannot disobey it; if you leave him unsupported in mid-air, he has no more choice about falling than a stone has. As an organism, he is subjected to various biological laws which he cannot disobey any more than an animal can. That is, he cannot disobey those laws which he shares with other things; but the law which is peculiar to his human nature, the law he does not share with animals or vegetables or inorganic things, is the one he can disobey if he chooses.

So, the unavoidable truth is this: the Boise student quoted earlier could have just as easily decided to override her sense of justice but she did not. Unlike the law of gravity, which cannot be disobeyed, other laws of nature can and often are. A person may know in his or her nature that something is inherently wrong, but decide to do it anyway. Many people fall into this latter camp when it comes to ignoring the liabilities of copyright infringement and pirating music and movies. People like Falkvinge and The Pirate Bay followers aggressively override their own sense of justice and fair play. They make a conscious decision to ignore previously established societal mores and choose, instead, to obtain immediate gratification at society's expense.

This is perhaps the real reason copyright must be defended: people are making the choice to disobey the rules our Founding Fathers and later legislators and jurists developed. The fact that they make this choice to disobey the rules is not, however an indictment of the copyright system. It is rather a demise of something much more profound: it is a decline in the value we as a society place on original thought.

The devaluation of original thought is evident in the book, referenced earlier, titled *Against Intellectual Monopoly*, by Michele Boldrin and David Levine, when they state that one of the "greatest dangers" of the intellectual monopoly is the "wasteful effort to suppress competition and obtain special privileges," something they call "rent-seeking" behavior. This, of course, misses what we have seen as the components of the copyright monopoly: the effort to build a *marketplace of ideas* by giving incentives to creators and inventors to encourage creation. Thus, the element of competition, as well as the element of "rent," *i.e.*, incentive, are, in fact, crucial components in the construct our Forefathers developed for us. As we have seen, competition is not a "danger" in our copyright construction, it is one of the foundational principles helping us deliver a utilitarian end.

The encouraging news in all of this, then, is a trend can be altered. As long as we as a society continue to value original thoughts of creative minds, there is hope for copyright. In order to preserve original thought, our societal justice has to be grounded in the philosophy of our Founding Fathers that giving people a copyright in their original thoughts will provide an incentive for them to create works and those creations benefit society both. Most importantly, we have to remember the duality: these benefits occurs at the time of creation and subsequently when they fall into the public's grasp. Both elements are required to maintain a fertile continuum of thought.

The Mystic Web

Ideas can no more flow backward than can a river.

~Victor Hugo

*Originality is the one thing unoriginal
minds cannot feel the use of.*

~John Stuart Mill

As I started this book, so will I end it: I believe original ideas fuel the drive of human innovation toward the future. Current U.S. copyright law are designed to stimulate original thought, thereby providing a great benefit to society by continuing to weave new ideas into the tapestry of thought, *i.e.*, the continuum of thought.

To describe this idea more fully, it is apropos that I make use of an expressed thought from the public domain: I am adapting the words of a poem entitled *The Tapestry Weaver*, written by Rev. Anson G. Chester of Buffalo, New York. The poem first appeared in Volume 75 of the periodical, *Christian Advocate*, on August 15, 1900:

The thoughts of man are looms of Nature,
Let down from the place of the sun,
Wherein we are weaving always,
Till the mystic web is done.

Weaving blindly but weaving surely,
Each for himself his own ideas,
We may not see how the right side looks,
We can only weave and wait.

But looking above for the pattern,
No weaver need have fear,
Only let him look clear into heaven
The perfect pattern is there.

Assuming an average life span of around 67 years, excluding the first five, if a person meets on average one to three new people a day, this means the average person will encounter between 20-65,000 new people in the course of their lifetime. Whether you believe these encounters are random acts of chance or are arranged for a special purpose, it is probable a majority of those encounters will impact a person's life. In some instances the impact may be imperceptible, but at other times it will be significant.

One might legitimately inquire as to what these social interactions have to do with original thought? I say each person impacts your life, even if only in a small way, because I believe each person has within them the capability of producing original thoughts and those interactions are often the filter for originality as illustrated in our examples from Einstein. No, everyone is not a Leonardo da Vinci, a Thomas Jefferson, an Albert Einstein, or an Isaac Newton. But each person weaves into the tapestry of life his or her unique and original world view, a perspective shaped, in turn, by the people who are interwoven through the tapestry of their own life. The continuum of knowledge, then, is a patchwork quilt of generic ideas, original thoughts, and innovations.

This tapestry, then, is the origin of thought I talked about in regard to Einstein. Perhaps no other human in history could have produced the machinations of original thoughts that churned away in the brain of Einstein. Remember what Einstein said: *it is our intellectual experience that provides the unconscious fertilizer for original thought.*

Society's utilitarian interest in maintaining copyright law is to encourage the creation of these kinds of original thoughts. Original thought produces creative and innovative works and their fluid dissemination into the fertile continuum of knowledge, the tapestry of human thought, causes society to grow. In this way, these works ultimately benefit society more than they benefit the individual creator. The resulting works offer a dual benefit in as much as they benefit society both at the time of their creation and again when the works fall into the public domain.

Make no mistake about it, the works resulting from incentivized original thought fuel the engine of free expression in both instances, stimulating discussion and further thought, and allowing more people to put them into their own ideation, thereby generating new original thoughts. As the tapestry is woven over the course of time, it allows other people to "cast on" their original ideas and thoughts to the tapestry, sometimes without any awareness of the overall pattern emerging in the societal Zeitgeist. It is no wonder it is so easy to assume all ideas have been thought before, as the weave is so tight and often the thread is latched to some bare idea that was in the tapestry before.

The tapestry of thoughts has existed since humans uttered their first thoughts and continues to furl throughout our history. It will continue to unfurl long after we are gone. It does not matter that persons other than the creator are restricted from copying the original works by the copyright monopoly construct which is so demeaned in our society, since new creators are not restricted from forming and expressing their own innovations based on the thoughts in the continuum, thus weaving them into the tapestry.

It is because of this ability to build upon ideas in the continuum of thought in order to form new innovations that copyright law does not threaten our free speech rights in the least. To the degree there is a conflict, as we observed, our Founding Fathers believed the benefit to society resulting from these subsequent contributions to the continuum more than outweighed any detriment to free speech.

Rampant copyright infringement in the form of "free" digital downloads harms creators and threatens to weaken the threads of the tapestry. It threatens to destroy our continuum of thought. Piracy harms creators financially and it inhibits their ability to create, thus disincentivizing them. Piracy threatens to create a drought in the flow of the continuum. People may argue against the value of copyright for the purpose of providing incentive, but all it takes is a trip to any creative hub in the country to witness the diminished paychecks for those who created art in this decade to find a compelling counter argument. The trend among a few to diminish this function of copyright is in direct opposition to the utilitarian goals of our society, just as it is contrary to the intent of our Founding Fathers when they drafted the Constitution. If we continue to abolish the incentive, the continuum of thought will degenerate into a collage of previous expressions. Original ideas will die.

The trend can be diverted so long as the majority is willing to uphold societal values and refrain from stealing, whether it be physically shoplifting an iPhone or copying another's ideas, not so much because we want to obey the law, but because of our innate sense of justice and fairness: that the right thing to do is to reward the laborer with the fruits of his or her toil. Society applauds a homeowner who staves off a would-be burglar, even if the homeowner has to use deadly force in defending his physical property. Most in society recognize and applaud the right of the creative to equally defend their "homestead" of intellectual property and protect their rights, no matter what type of force is used.

We must elevate the value of the origins of an idea to its original perch. To do so inspires our sense of trust in society and gives us incentive to contribute, a concept explored thoroughly in Bruce Schneier's recent work, *Liars & Outliers*. It was our Founding Fathers who created the institution of copyright and it has worked well for over 200 years, because we trusted them. If we maintain belief in the protection of original thought expression, our inventors and creators can continue to achieve success and wealth through the revelation of their original thoughts and continue to weave a tapestry of original ideas. So long as society as a whole agrees to value their sense of justice, obeying the rules it has established by social contract, the rule remains a viable and valid motivator. Copyright remains a valuable construct and its benefits to society are without question. Our society will continue to thrive. The continuum of thought will progress.

On the Vanderbilt University's First Amendment Center website, LL Cool J is quoted as saying:

> This is our country. . . . [O]ur country has a lot of diversity. It has a lot of different people in it who have a lot of different ideas. And all of those ideas deserve to be heard. All of them.

As long as there are those who are willing to defend the origins of an idea, the monopoly created by our Founding Fathers for original expressions will remain an engine of free expression, giving benefits to society. It will perpetuate the continuum of thought, which is fertile soil for the origin of an idea. New creators will draw from the concepts and ideas embedded in the Zeitgeist of humanity and be inspired to create new expressions. The force of their labor and creativity on these ideas should be rewarded, so the infinite möbius of free expression continues.

References

Anthony, Scott, *How Do You Create a Culture of Innovation,* http://www.fastcodesign.com/1669657/how-do-you-create-a-culture-of-innovation.

Bently, Lionel, Suthersanen, Uma, Torremans, Paul *Global Copyright: Three Hundred Years Since the Statute of Anne, from 1709 to Cyberspace,* Edward Elgar Publishing, Inc. 2010.

Bohannan, Christina, *Copyright Harm and Reform,* Iowa Law Review Bulletin, Vol. 96, No. 13, 2010.

Bohannan, Christina, *Copyright Harm and the First Amendment,* University of Iowa, 2009.

Boldrin & Levine, *Against Intellectual Monopoly,* 2007.

Collingswood, R.G., *The Principles of Art,* 1938.

Ely, Jr. James W., *Property Rights in America,* Prepared for Hillsdale College's Free Market Forum, "The Role of Markets and Governments in Pursuing the Common Good", Panel Topic: "21st Century Challenges to Property Rights," September 26, 2008.

Foley, John P. Ed., The Jefferson Cyclopedia, *A Comprehensive Collection of the Views of Thomas Jefferson,* Funk & Wagnalls Company, New York, 1900.

Ford, Paul Leicester, Ed., *The Works of Thomas Jefferson,* The Knickerbocher Press, G.P. Putnam's Sons, New York, 1904.

Hafer, Catherine, *On the Origins of Property Rights: Conflict and Production in the State of Nature,* October 2003.

Hettinger, Edwin C., *Justifying intellectual property*, Philosophy and Public Affairs, Vol. 18, No. 1, Winter 1989.

Hunt, Gaillard, *The Writings of James Madison* (1910).

Johnson, Samuel. *Dictionary of the English Language* (4th ed 1775)
Lessig, Lawrence, *Free Culture: The Nature and Future of Creativity*, Penguin 2005.

Lessig, Lawrence, *ReMix: Making Art and Commerce Thrive in the Hybrid Economy*, Penguin Press, 2008.

Litman, Jessica, *Real Copyright Reform*, 96 IOWA L. REV. 1 (2010).

Looney, J., ed., *Papers of Thomas Jefferson.* 2009.

Samuelson, Pamela, *Legally Speaking: Too Many Copyrights?* Communications of the ACM, Vol. 54, No. 7, July 2011.

Schneier, Bruce. *Liars and Outliers: Enabling the Trust that Society Needs to Thrive.* Wiley & Sons, New York (2012).

Solberg, Thorvald, *Copyright in Congress 1789-1904* (1905).

Taylor, Quentin, Online Library of Liberty, 2011. http://oll.libertyfund.org/readinglists/print/194-major_political_thinkers_ plato _to_mill

Washington, H.A., Ed., *The Writings of Thomas Jefferson, Being his Autobiography, Correspondence, Reports, Messages, Addresses, and Other Writings, Official and Private*, Vol. VII, Derby & Jackson, New York, 1859.

Webster's American Dictionary of the English Language (1828) (reprinted 2010).

ABOUT THE AUTHOR

Barry Neil Shrum, Esquire is an entertainment attorney who has been practicing law for over 16 years, representing some of the biggest name in the music and entertainment industries as well as numerous other clients in the creative and Internet sectors. Mr. Shrum also teaches copyright, entertainment law, licensing, and Cyberlaw at the prestigious Mike Curb School of Music Business at Belmont University. He currently lives in the suburbs of Music City USA (Nashville) where he enjoys spending time with his family and watching his son play tennis.

Made in the USA
Columbia, SC
17 November 2018